Gentle Ways in Japan

GENTLE WAYS

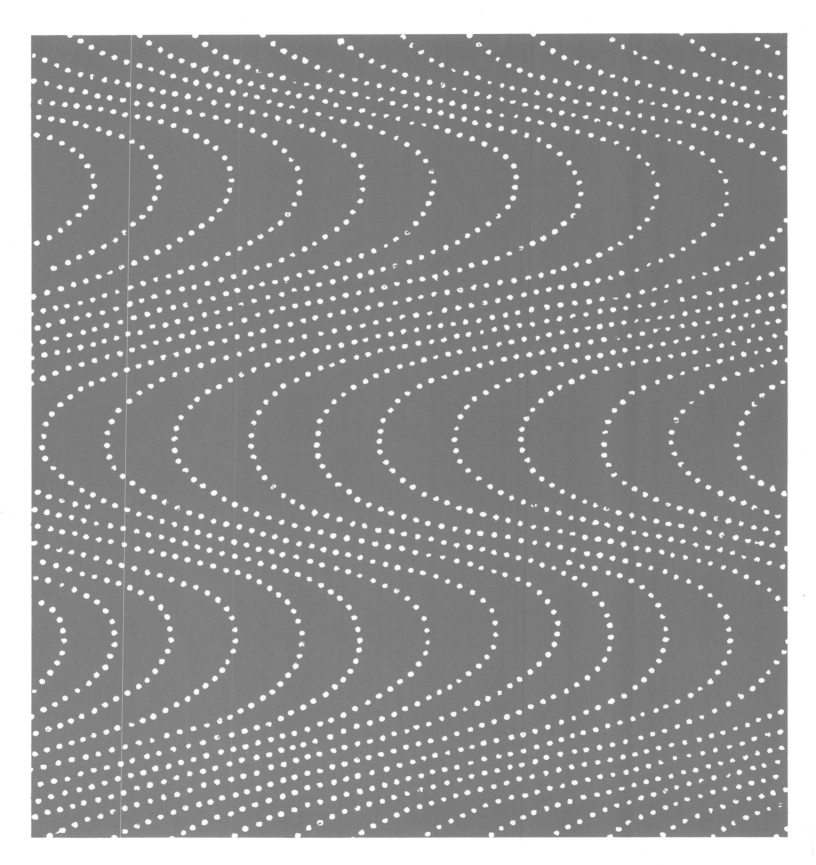

IN JAPAN

A Photographic Study of the Familiar

Text & Photos by
GERARD P. SHELDON

Introduction by
STUART D. B. PICKEN

Saville Photo Arts Publishing
Tiburon / San Francisco, California

Saville Photo Arts Publishing
1640 Tiburon Blvd.
Tiburon, California   94920

All photographs are by Gerard P. Sheldon
with the exception of PANELS 31R, 32L,
34L, and 40R; see Acknowledgments.

Design & Production: Christensen & Son Design
Composition: G & S Typesetters, Inc.
Separation & Printing: Dai Nippon

Library of Congress Catalog Card Number 89-090649

ISBN 0-9621904-0-3

Acknowledgments

THIS VOLUME IS DEDICATED to my wife, Kana, a unique person whose gentle, kind and loving ways have given me during the past thirty-four years a more limpid vision of life's essential than all the experience gathered before. She is the central inspiration of this study, and I thank her most warmly for her unequalled patience and advice during the many months it took to compile the photographs and finish this book.

My deep gratitude goes to Mrs. Virginia Watkins-Josselyn, a life-long expert in Japanese art and customs, for her generous and selfless assistance in the revision of the text and the final selection of the photographs. Dr. Franklyn Josselyn, Professor Emeritus of the Philosophy of Religions, now teaching the History of Western Ideas at Doshisha University in Kyoto, has also revised the manuscript and I greatly appreciate his helpful suggestions. I am more than thankful to him for writing the Foreword to this book.

In addition, I am highly grateful to the Rev. Professor Stuart D. B. Picken of International Christian University in Tokyo for his many useful ideas in the genesis of this work and more particularly for writing the Introduction to this volume as well as revising the manuscript. Moreover, Professor Picken has been most kind in giving me permission to reproduce three photographs in Chapter III [PANELS 31R, 34L, 40R] from his book, *Shinto—Japan's Spiritual Roots*. Photo credit is given here to the photographers working with Kodansha International Ltd. in the publication of Dr. Picken's book on Shinto as follows: Fine Photo Agency for *omiyamairi* [PANEL 31R]; Haga Hideo for *misogi* [PANEL 34L]; and Photo International Agency for *ohanami* [PANEL 40R]. I also most indebted to Meiji Jingu, Tokyo, for allowing me to reproduce their photo of *hichi-go-san* [PANEL 32L]. Permissions were obtained from these four photographic sources for reproducing the above numbered pictures solely in the publication of *Gentle Ways in Japan* and are herewith thankfully acknowledged.

Finally, my heartfelt appreciation is given to the many anonymous individuals—men, women and children—shown in these pages, and whom I have no way of thanking personally. Their faces, hidden in many snapshots and slides, came to brilliant life in these enlarged photographs thanks to the great skills of Newell Color Lab and Faulkner Color Lab in San Francisco, to whom I remain very much indebted.

GERARD P. SHELDON, M.D.
Tiburon, California
August 1988

Foreword

WESTERNERS who have lived in Japan for many years are reminded by this remarkable book of the gentle strength and inner beauty of the Japanese people. Westerners who merely tour through Japan having little time to experience the deeper meanings of Japanese behavior are here given glimpses beneath the surface of customs, traditions and places.

Dr. Sheldon's insights are the product of his sensitivity and fascination with the inner spirit of the Japanese people. His insight is also derived from his long experience as the husband of a Japanese woman who has taught him to see and hear and understand the inner meaning of Japanese practices and places. He knows how the people relate to each other in quiet, subtle ways so different from his own Western nurture. He is also aware of the sacred energy in rocks, rivers, waterfalls and nature, even where there are no shrines and temples. He perceives the power of a small roadside Buddha where small rocks and stones are used in acts of prayer in remembrance of children. He sees the man who is cleansed by rinsing his mouth at a Shinto fountain, and the pregnant woman who is strengthened in a simple, quiet act of purification at a shrine. He knows the Japanese ways of experiencing the realities of the divine.

Thus his pictures reveal with extraordinary clarity how the Japanese behave in familiar places like little streetside shops and in special places like historic temples. His camera catches the ways in which ordinary people express their inner feelings in ordinary situations. He catches the power of a seemingly casual gesture and the quite beauty of a momentary social interchange because he knows what to look for and how to help others see the inner dimensions of life in Japan.

His words accompanying each pair of photographs put *Gentle Ways* into historic, geographic and ethic perspective while emphasizing important aspects of Japanese life. As the eye and talent of an artist reveals the uniqueness of special moments in ways seldom noticed by casual observers, so the pictures and words of this book portray the special grace and inner beauty of Japan's people and places.

DR. FRANKLYN JOSSELYN
Professor Emeritus, Philosophy of Religions,
Occidental College, Los Angeles
Visiting Professor, History of Western Ideas,
Doshisha University, Kyoto
Kyoto, Japan
April 1, 1988

Chronology*

Japan	China
JOMON ?—300 B.C.	CHOU DYNASTY 1027—256 B.C.
YAYOI 300 B.C.—A.D. 300	HAN DYNASTY 206 B.C.—A.D. 220
KOFUN (Tumulus) 300—552	SIX DYNASTIES 250—589
ASUKA (SUIKO) PERIOD 552—645	
Important rulers:	
Empress Suiko 593—628	SUI DYNASTY 518—618
Prince Shotoku, Regent 593—622	
NARA PERIOD 645—794	TANG DYNASTY 618—906
Early Nara (Hakuko) 646—710	
Late Nara (Tempyo) 710—794	
Important rulers:	
Shomu 724—747	
Empress Koken 749—758	
HEIAN PERIOD 794—1185	
Early Heian (Jogan) 794—897	
Late Heian (Fujiwara) 897—1185	FIVE DYNASTIES 907—960
	NORTHERN SUNG 960—1127
KAMAKURA PERIOD 1185—1333	SOUTHERN SUNG 1127—1279
Important Shogun:	YUAN DYNASTY 1288—1368
Minamoto Yorimoto 1192—1199	
MUROMACHI (ASHIKAGA) 1333—1573	
Important Shoguns:	
Ashikaga Yoshimitsu 1368—1394	MING DYNASTY 1368—1644
Ashikaga Yoshimasa 1449—1473	
MOMOYAMA PERIOD 1573—1615	
Important rulers:	
Oda Nobunaga 1573—1582	
Toyotomi Hideyoshi 1586—1598	
Tokugawa Ieyasu 1600—1616	
EDO PERIOD 1615—1868	CHING DYNASTY 1644—1912
MEIJI PERIOD 1868—1912	

*Adapted from Stern, H. P.: *Birds, Bees, Blossoms and Bugs: The Nature of Japan*, H. N. Abrams, N.Y. 1976, and Trubner et al.: *Asiatic Art in the Seattle Museum*, Seattle Art Museum 1973.

Contents

Preface

I.

JAPAN'S PHENOMENAL postwar development resulted in a huge industrial and technological complex, sometimes referred to as "Japan Inc.", which places it second to the United States as the world's leading economic power. There is also another Japan variously called "old" or "premodern," "real" or "folkloric," "feudal" or "rural" which reaches back two thousand years to the mists of legend. This volume is a photographic study of some aspects of this other Japan that have been shaped by centuries of homogeneity and custom, and which are called here Gentle Ways. These pertain to the familiar, seen mostly among women and children, old and retired people, farmers, artists and others who are under less severe rules and constraints than men in the business and the professional worlds. For a clearer perception of what the two Japans are and what relation exists between them the reader is referred to the Documentary Appendix.

The Japanese character is fashioned early in life by three sets of cultural influences loosely intertwined, but never very far from the surface: Shinto, Confucian and Buddhist. There is first "a gentle feeling for life and nature" derived from ancient Shinto, a simple cult of primitive gods—still an active religion—which embodies a set of beliefs, traditions and customs at the very root of Japanese cultural life. This has been studied in depth by Picken, the foremost Western expert on Shinto,[6] and will be considered further in Chapter III on Customs. It must be stressed here that Shinto as perceived in Japan today has little to do with the frightful militaristic overtones given it by the war clique during Japan's darkest years from 1931 to 1945.

While Confucianism and its precepts have been central to life in China for centuries, what was retained in Japan were certain Confucian values which still permeate society today. These values center on loyalty in interpersonal relationships, respect for elders, belief in education and hard work, as well as public confidence in the excellence and moral basis of Government.[7]

The Buddhist influence in Japan, where it is quite different from its origins in India, China and other Asian civilizations, has been very well outlined, again by Picken.[9] "Of the three marks of existence, the first, that all life is permeated by suffering, has left its imprint on the Japanese as their aptitude to patiently endure unpleasant experiences. The second and the third marks of existence, flowing from the first, are all but incomprehensible to the Western mind steeped in individualism and self assertiveness: They state that existence of the self is just an illusion, and that since everything changes all the time, nothing is permanent anyway. The Japanese have translated this concept of the non-importance of the self into the importance of the group as the framework of human identity."[9] The nature of that group may be better understood in terms of three cardinal features of Japanese life: harmony and homogeneity; persistence of old, traditional social structures; the group as a source of social and emotional security [see Documentary Appendix].[5,10]

II.

Almost everyone who works in Japan Inc.'s vast industrial complex returns at night to a world dominated by women—the undisputed masters of the home in Japan—the world of children, old people, and family. This "other Japan" differs so markedly from the world of Western women and families because even today, it is permeated to an unusual degree by age-old customs and patterns. Everyone employed in the "new Japan" has his roots in this "other Japan", where he was born and raised and where—no matter how important and powerful he may have become—he acquired the basic thought pattern of the Japanese of long ago, with a certain innocent and cheerful gentleness hidden somewhere in his psyche. While formal behavior is bound by innumerable constraints of rank and obligations, the Japanese innermost personality remains in need of *amae*, the ancestral concept of "looking for and giving affection."[4] What is true for the work-group in Japan applies also to every other group or association, since all derive from the basic concept of informal household structure discussed in the Appendix. Thus, it may be said that the "modern Japan" Westerners first see on landing in Tokyo or in Osaka is the same as the "other or old Japan", since the former derives from the latter, and the apparent only conceals the real.

One Japanese trait that perhaps primes all others is adaptability. Japan Inc.'s enormous size may represent the titanic attempt made by the nation as a whole to adapt to the post-industrial technological world, and perhaps even to absorb it. Twice before in its long history Japan faced such severe challenges. The first time came in the seventh century A.D. with the massive invasion of Chinese culture and civilization which lasted for 300 years. The Japanese took what they liked from this overwhelming influx of foreign influences, adapted what they wanted to their needs and discarded the rest. Their success in this endeavor was so great that it culminated in the brilliant Heian period, a span of four centuries highlighted by extraordinary accomplishments in art, literature and decorative splendor—all essentially Japanese—so that it became the nation's true classical age which has remained the fountainhead of its civilization.

The second extreme challenge which faced Japan was the tumultuous onslaught of Western customs and industrial methods at the beginning of the Meiji period in 1868, when the Tokugawa shogunate ended Japan's long isolation of nearly three hundred years. The adaptation to that challenge was also prodigiously successful, not "by changing the traditional social and political structure of Japan but by utilizing it."[10] However this rapid modernization was marred by the limitless ambition of the lower rank samurai who assumed the country's leadership during the Meiji period.[11] The wanton Russo-Japanese War at the turn of the century as well as the tragic and murderous invasion of Manchuria were nothing but megalomanic power-plays by the Meiji leaders. Unfortunately, these were the forerunners of the criminal military clique that came on the scene in 1931 and brought about the atomic cataclysm of 1945, thus terminating Japan's age of folly.

But with the first atomic bombs came not only the American occupation and McArthur's benevolent rule, but also the first computer and the dawn of the technological age. This confronted Japan with its third, and perhaps most difficult historical challenge. The necessity arose not only to navigate again on uncharted seas, but to live with an occupant, now friendly as the Chinese had once been. Perhaps in time, this occupant could be equalled, and maybe even "outdistanced by peaceful means"! This was certainly not in the minds of the stunned Japanese of 1945, but the course of events has shown that modernization and adaptation again succeeded beyond all expectations. It is important to remember that in the Meiji period Japan never really became Westernized, and after World War II it did not become Americanized. In both cases, however, vast mutations occurred "without any structural change in the time-honored basic social configuration."[10] Everything adapted by the Japanese throughout their history undergoes a peculiar metamorphosis[12] so that the finished product is generally a far cry from the original model.

III.

The countercultural revolution of the sixties in the West did send ripples through Japan: There were student revolts in major universities, criminal activities by Red Army terrorists, even some violence in the schools; but as is traditionally the case in Japan, homogeneity and peace prevailed over anarchy. Appropriate group measures taken at various levels of government and public life seem to have defused what could have been major upheavals, and general order seems to prevail again. Twelve years ago Reischauer wrote: "Japanese society is remarkable for its homogeneity, orderliness and adherence to strict patterns . . . As compared to others. Japan seems relatively stable . . . It is not rent by sharp cleavages, but is almost monotonously uniform . . . In a fast changing society, no one can say that present conditions of stability and apparent contentedness will last forever. Only time will tell, but at present Japan can be considered one of the most successful modern societies."[5] Twelve years later, it still is.

The network of "small society relationships" which binds the Japanese together in an infinity of small groups is an essentially informal affair. It often involves warm human bonds and frequently derives from the familiar. It is the familiar, and more specifically the "gentle" aspects of this cohesive life pattern which I have endeavored to capture on film for the past 35 years, and which I am presenting here in 99 PANELS grouped in five chapters. Each chapter corresponds to an important aspect of the familiar in daily life: **Children, Women, Customs, Country Life, City Life.** Each PANEL consists of two facing photographs on related subjects with an explanatory text sufficiently clear as to exclude reference to other pages as much as possible. This entails a minimum of repetition, but it has the marked advantage that any PANEL in the book may be viewed on its own as a single unit, without any given order, for the reader's maximum enjoyment. Supplemental reading of the section's introduction, the Preface and the Documentary Appendix may then take place if so desired. Similarly, each chapter attempts to be a well-defined entity, but can be read independently of the others.

I believe that many of the Gentle Ways depicted in these photographs form an integral part of the Japanese ethos. They illustrate some aspects of the "dense social matrix" which so far has helped Japan to cushion the dehumanizing blows of the technological age better than most other nations.

Introduction

DR. SHELDON paints a sensitive and sympathetic portrait of social and family life in Japan that at first sight seems either out of place or even irrelevant to the image of contemporary Japan that is most frequently portrayed in business journals, travel magazines or the popular press. Japan the economic giant is a land of noise and grime, overcrowding and traffic jams, "examination hell" and cramped housing, suicide and social pressures, to name but a few of the problems which Japan's critics take great pleasure in publicizing (as if other industrial societies were free of these problems). A brief trip to Tokyo might indeed confirm that these symptoms exist. But such a trip would be very brief and would result in a highly superficial understanding of Japan and the Japanese. It is of course this type of reporting on Japan that the mass media have specialized in for the decades following the 1960s, when Japan's post-war emergence began to catch the attention of the West. Japan-bashing then targeted on Japan's pollution problems which, bad then, still did not compare with conditions at the same time in London or Glasgow (where I spent my school years) where fog and filth had been accepted as a life hazard since the early nineteenth century. Japan in a mere twenty-years has come a long way towards an improved environment although it may yet be far from ideal. Japan-bashing today concentrates on housing problems, the cost of living and trade practices. Again, the short term observer will find plenty of ammunition to fill his notepad which can be used to fire salvos on Japan's economy, Japanese society and the "enigmatic" or "unscrupulous" Japanese.

While no society is perfect, Japan receives more than her fair share of bad treatment at the hands of writers, reporters and journalists. It was almost fashionable in the 1970s for certain kinds of journalists to visit Japan for two weeks and write a nasty book exposing the country's weaknesses and predicting how soon it would be before the great social explosion took place. It is for this reason that Dr. Sheldon's book, *Gentle Ways*, is a welcome contribution as a corrective to these negative images which are so pervasive and difficult to refute with words alone. The author has spent more than three full decades visiting Japan on a regular basis. In his photographic record, he covers precisely the thirty years of controversy I have just discussed, and he shows a different Japan from the one the media have depicted ad nauseam.

Dr. Sheldon speaks and argues with a camera, by producing over thirty years an illustrated documentation of the simple thesis that behind the dynamics of a harsh industrial environment and a tough commercial lifestyle, there still survives an older Japan, a gentler Japan and a more human Japan. Indeed, Dr. Sheldon goes further and argues that without the existence of this other Japan in the background, the Japan most visible to the observer could not have succeeded as well as it has. It is the author's central contention that Japan's unique ability to adapt to overwhelming change while keeping close to its spiritual and cultural roots is the very reason why the Japanese have coped with the dehumanizing effects of the technological civilization far better than other industrial nations. This is a bold thesis, but a thesis that is worth consideration because it helps to explain in part something of the paradoxical character of Japanese culture, Japanese society and the Japanese people which any astute observer comes to recognize very quickly.

Anyone looking through the book with an open mind must be fascinated by the tremendous sense of identity between faces and behaviour depicted in these photographs of thirty years ago and those of yesterday. Patterns of continuity in manners, gestures and expressions are reminders of the Japan that does not easily change. The trained eye will recognize changes in the fashion of clothes, old road signs or advertisements that have changled their style. The externals are indeed temporal, ephemeral but very much peripheral to the deep heart that is timeless, unchanging and central to the life of a unique people. Dr. Sheldon has captured all this and more with skill as well as feeling. Indeed it is as though the soul of Lafcadio Hearn had been released with a camera to prove that things he said in the nineteenth century might still be valid a century later simply because they will always be true.

Dr. Sheldon is himself a kind and gentle man who has seen and experienced the best of Japan's kind and gentle ways. It is refreshing to look at Japan through eyes that are free of cynicism and negation and to see the good that is there. The essence of Shinto lies in its belief in the restoring power of endless natural renewal through purification. Something of this is caught in the author's work and something of that spirit is in the photographer, otherwise he would have never been able to capture the moods and the emotions which he does.

Gentle Ways is a nostalgic journey through an older Japan that still exists for those who have eyes to see it. It is part of the hidden secret of Japan now, and Dr. Sheldon has done well to make it so visible. If a picture be worth a thousand words, we have thousands of eloquent words dedicated to a more profound understanding of the mysteries of Japan than that presented by many of the academic and pseudo-academic writers. It is a book that will generate both pleasure and enlightenment, a rarely found combination, and one that is also a tribute to the efforts and insights of its author. It has been my privilege to see its creation and to make a few observations on how its case might be strengthened here and there, a privilege which I have deeply appreciated.

I wish *Gentle Ways* great success and look forward to the next venture from the eyes and the pen of this physician who is a friend, a classicist of the old school and a man who at the center of his being is truly and profoundly human. I can offer no better compliment to either the author or the book.

STUART D. B. PICKEN, M.A., B.D., PH.D., F.R.A.S.
Rev. Professor of Philosophy and Comparative Ethics
International Christian University, Tokyo, Japan
June 1, 1988

CHILDREN

JAPANESE MYTHOLOGY revolves around three fundamental concepts: Deities (or *kami*), Nature, and Man. These are intimately related in the Shinto religious tradition, which has been so well studied by Picken.[6] In Shinto, "*kami* are not superhuman dwellers of a distant heavenly realm, but deities close to the world of daily life. A *kami* . . . is anything which can inspire in human beings a feeling of awe, reverence, or mystery . . . It may be expressed as a love of nature but also . . . as a sense of reverence before life's power and vitality."[6]

To the Japanese, "the very islands on which he dwells are elder children procreated by the gods who are his own ancestors." In contrast with the West where the Hebrew and Christian traditions both view nature as "inimical and unredeemed by divine grace," the Japanese believe that "nature is kind and a mother's bosom to her children, the people."[14,6] For Watsuji, who studied national character as a function of climate, "man in Japan has never been torn from the familiar circle of animals, flowers and rocks. The Japanese likes to tune his inner life to the rhythm of the seasons, submitting to the powers of nature . . . feeling most free when yielding to her moods." This closeness to nature seems to be rooted in remote childhood experiences and remains with the Japanese throughout their lives.[14]

Shinto's third important concept, Man, now appears "not as a creature of the gods, but as a child born of the *kami* . . ." Thus in Japanese mythology, human nature remains innocent, and despite possible unworthy actions, "does not emerge from the Garden of Eden corrupted and radically evil."[6] It is this mythological view of nature as an infinite and benevolent source of life that Singer compares to "the mother not separated from her children by a painful process of weaning. For years the child is strapped to his mother's back . . . sharing in a half-drowsy state her warmth and her rhythm . . . feeling sheltered and close to the maternal body"[11] [PANELS 10,22]. Perhaps it is this very closeness to the mother's body, when securely fastened to her back for so long, that gives the Japanese his remarkable acceptance of fate, his horror of isolation and his usually wonderful recollection of childhood.

By the same token, it has "often been said that Japan is a children's paradise." This is best observed by strolling in cities, or sightseeing spots, or in the countryside. Probably nowhere else can so many children of all ages be seen on any day of the year; always in groups, large or small, except when running late for school [PANEL 7], well groomed and well behaved, apparently cheerful and happy [PANELS 4–6,8,12]. Little children are particularly wonderful, and have often a unique, radiant quality like nature at dawn on a clear summer day, "a soothing and refreshing source of life" [PANELS 1–3,63L]. Similarly, the "freshness of the ocean at sunrise portrays two important Shinto values, brightness and purity, the ideals of a civilization in which the good and the beautiful are one."[6] In Maurice Chevalier's famous song, little girls may "grow up in the most delightful way"; in Japan they are most delightful in early childhood, remain so throughout their school years and often indefinitely.

Small children, and "especially boys, more so if it is a first-born son, are almost free from any restraint. The child may do as it likes; it is very rarely scolded." Even on the street, the child may shout, run or climb as it wishes. If admonition comes, it is mostly gentle and without anger.[11] Most important is that Japanese little kids are treated and act like children, not as adults. Children in Japan have not been robbed of their childhood and do not lose their innocent radiance as early as in the West, where they are often treated like grownups and may acquire a plastic patina and adult mannerisms long before their time.

As the Japanese child grows up, the demands placed upon it become increasingly more severe. The pressures start to build up in junior high school and sometimes earlier. The well known "examination hell" which precedes entrance to top universities requires exhaustive and lengthy preparation. When the student finally graduates from the university and has cleared the last hurdle of getting a job (often after another examination given by the hiring company), he has developed "a mask made up of discipline, tradition, self-restraint, diffidence." Until his retirement, he will probably put in a ten to twelve hour day, including two to three hours commuting time. His freedom of action has now been permanently curtailed by the multiple constraints of adult existence.[11]

For the rest of his life, the Japanese's "sense of complete enjoyment" will remain embedded in the "irrevocable past of his childhood where he had complete freedom to do as he liked, that blissful state where he was the center of the Universe." The Japanese form of revolution has always been renewal or renovation. "Man is good and no harm is done if he follows his impulses, for it was thus that he gained and retained the love and admiration of his parents, the kindest and strongest beings he ever knew."[11] This childhood Nirvana remains at the foundation of the country's collective unconsciousness. It is forever summoned by the innocent radiance of Japanese children and it is that very radiance which the following photographs are trying to portray.

PANEL I

"It has often been said that Japan is a children's paradise. Small boys, and especially first born sons, are almost free from any restraint . . . Japanese children are spared the baneful 'You must not' to such a degree that they are termed the real gods of the country. . . . They are the center of the house and of the nation. Clad in the brightest of colors they are the only people in Japan to whom freedom of action is granted without stint."¹¹ The photo above was taken in Okayama's Korakuen Park in 1985. Okayama is less than an hour by fast train (Shinkansen) from Kobe and is the ancient castle stronghold of Ikeda, an important provincial lord of the Edo period.

4

The extraordinary little girl seen running here was photographed in the gardens of the Meiji Shrine in Tokyo (April 1988). The Meiji Shrine is one of the holiest centers of pilgrimage in Japan, and it attracts huge crowds yearly. It is dedicated to Emperor Meiji and his wife in remembrance of their remarkable achievements which so impressed the nation that the original shrine—in pure Shinto style—was built soon after their deaths and was inaugurated in 1920 with a celebration of unprecedented scale. The grounds of the shrine, known as the Inner Garden, are exceptionally tranquil and beautiful. They cover nearly 180 acres in the heart of Tokyo.[20]

5

PANEL 2   Probably nowhere else can so many children of all ages be seen on any day of the year as in Japan. School children, always in groups, are taken on sightseeing and recreational tours to parks and places of interest throughout the length and width of the country. Both these photographs are also taken at Okayama's Korakuen Park in 1985. Above are grade school children on an outing walking in order, and on the right are little girls on another school excursion having a picnic lunch on the lawn.

They all sit in small groups on neatly laid out blankets and eat their lunches from *obento* boxes usually containing rice, some fish, a variety of pickled vegetables, and perhaps a fruit in season. They drink hot green tea or juices from thermos bottles. Teachers are sitting together, and tree leaves are beginning to turn yellow. The four little girls in the foreground seem to be having a great time.

Korakuen Park is one of the three most celebrated parks in Japan, the other two being the Kenrokuen at Kanazawa, and the Kairakuen at Mito. The garden, which covers about 22 acres and was laid out in 1786 by Lord Ikeda, features pavilions, ponds, cascades, magnificent trees and graceful contours.[20]

PANEL 3

Little children are particularly wonderful in Japan. They have often a unique radiant quality, like nature at dawn on a clear summer day, "a soothing and refreshing source of life".[11] Japanese mythology revolves around three concepts: gods (*kami*), Nature and Man. In Shinto belief, "man appears not as a creature of God, but as a child born of the *kami*".[6] The little girl above is completely absorbed with her mother's camera in a small noodle restaurant in Nara.

The cute girl on the right is giving all her attention to a calligraphy contest being held on a mobile box carried by a hapless student, according to some remote custom. The contest is taking place on May 5 (a national holiday in Japan) just outside the temple of Nison-in, a most ancient Tendai sanctuary founded in the middle of the eighth century in a lovely maple grove near Arashiyama, a beautiful wooded Kyoto suburb. (Both pictures were taken in 1988.)

8

PANEL 4

High school children on an outing at Nishi-Honganji in 1954 [*above*]. "This is one of the finest temples in Kyoto and is the headquarters of the Jodo-Shinshu Buddhist sect founded in the twelfth century by Shinran. He was a disciple of Honen—founder of the then larger Jodo sect—and he introduced married priesthood by wedding the daughter of a former Fujiwara Minister. Shinran was subsequently exiled but returned to Kyoto in 1235 and developed a large following. The Jodo-Shinshu sect thus discarded celibate priesthood, abstinence from meat and other ascetic practices and claimed salvation by faith in Amida, who is involved in the ubiquitous incantation 'Namu Amida Butsu'. The new sect encountered many difficulties and moved several times. It finally was allowed to build its headquarters on the present site by Toyotomi Hideyoshi at the end of the seventeenth century. The temple burned down in 1617 and has since been restored" while the Jodo-Shin sect became the largest in the country".[20]

The Kyoto Kaikan [*right*] is a huge modern entertainment center in Kyoto close to the Heian Shrine. The grade school children shown in the Kaikan's courtyard in 1987 are carried away at the sight of a foreigner (*gaijin*) taking their picture and while chanting "Hello" in a wide variety of tones, make the Churchillian sign of "V" for victory. This sign may signify either glee or greeting but in any case it is friendly and is made by younger children everywhere in Japan. In the children's eyes, all Caucasians are Americans and are usually well received. The high school children shown on the left thirty-three years earlier are both older and considerably more subdued.

10

PANEL 5 "Throughout their lives the Japanese's sense of complete enjoyment will remain embedded in the irrevocable past of his childhood, where he had complete freedom to do as he liked. That blissful state where he was the center of the Universe".[11] This childhood Nirvana remains at the foundation of the country's collective unconsciousness, and is forever summoned up by the innocent radiance of little children.

Both photographs were taken in Kyoto in 1954. Above are three small girls washing a dog in the Shirakawa Canal, while four others and a lady passerby look on. On the right, two boys are going to catch butterflies past a *torii* close to the Temple of Chio-in. The cut of their short pants well suggests the immediate post-World War II period.

PANEL 6

Here is a large group of grade school children in 1955, in front of the Todai-ji in Nara. This temple is the headquarters of the Kegon Buddhist sect, now nearly extinct but the oldest sect in Nara, imported from China in the sixth century. The Todai-ji was built from 745–752 by Shomu, the forty-fifth Emperor of Japan, who had been overwhelmed by the greatness of the Daibutsu (the Varocaina Buddha in Sanskrit) and wanted to spread his glory worldwide. That Buddha was compared "to the sun whose light of wisdom offers salvation to all beings in the Universe and reaches to the darkest corners of the world without leaving a shadow". The Great Buddha was cast several times before reaching his present shape and remains the largest bronze statue in the world. The Great Hall (Daibutsuden) built to protect it was one of the original seven great Buddhist temples in Nara. It burned down three times—in 1180, 1567, and 1914—and its actual size is two-thirds of the original one, yet the height of 166 feet remains the same. It is also the largest wooden building known on this planet and is registered as a National Treasure.[20]

14

The grade school girls here were seen in 1955 passing under a *torii* at Hakone Shrine, a large Shinto shrine in Central Japan secluded on a densely-wooded hillside arising from the shore of Lake Hakone which is a resort area near Myanoshita. "The shrine is well known as the place where Minamoto Yorimoto took refuge after a defeat at the hands of the Taira clan, with whom he fought for many years, to finally emerge the victor and start the Kamakura shogunate in 1192. The Shrine Festival is held each year on the night of July 31 on boats in the middle of the lake with thousands of lighted lanterns being floated from the shore".[20]

15

PANEL 7   Japanese children are mostly well groomed and well behaved in public. They are rarely seen yelling or fighting in
the streets. They are usually in groups except when running to or coming back from school (*both pictures*). As the
Japanese child grows up, the demands of society become
increasingly severe. The pressures start to build up in junior high school and sometimes earlier. The severe
preparation for entrance examinations to the top universities, if successful, is followed by four years in which
sports and social contacts can finally take place. These are
probably the only years before retirement in which the
Japanese will not have to put in a ten to twelve hour day.
"When the student finally graduates from the university, he
has developed a mask made up of discipline, tradition, self-
restraint, diffidence . . . His freedom of action is progres-
sively diminished by inhibitions, rules, taboos, and the
multiple constraints of adult life."[11]

16

Both pictures are taken in 1981 in Momoyama-minami-guchi (Peach-Hill-South-Exit), a large suburb of Kyoto well known for the tumulus-type burial mounds of Emperor Meiji and his consort. They are resting in a vast and sober enclosure surrounded by three fences made of cypress wood. This mausoleum is reached by an impressive flight of 230 stone steps and lies on the hill where "Hideyoshi, the last great ruler before the Tokugawa, once built his famous castle".[20]

PANEL 8

The delightful little girl above, with a small doll hanging from her school bag, is at the corner of Nijo and Kiyamachi Streets in Kyoto on her way to the Nijo Bridge. She is a few steps behind her two friends (not shown) and has some of the wonderful radiance so often seen in small Japanese children.

The cheerful children at right are just returning from a school excursion to Hiroshima's War Memorial Park in 1985. They have probably no real perception of the catastrophic disaster so well documented in the Atomic Bomb Museum, partially viewed in the background, which they have just seen. The visitor is greeted to that museum by this sober foreword inscribed on a white wall near the entrance in both Japanese and English and reproduced here word for word:

We believe that there are many today who either lack the knowledge or else are ignorant of the incredible heavy casualties that an atomic bomb could bring about. The Museum hopes to speak in behalf of the 200,000 victims' voiceless voices, the witness of history, and appeal to the people in the world the bare facts of what happened when the atomic bomb was dropped in Hiroshima.

18

PANEL 9 Both photographs show little girls all dressed up in multicolored traditional kimonos for the New Year celebration on January 1, 1955. They are seen in front of a general store promoting pens of all kinds, secondhand books and many other things in a small square of the seaside village of Kanazawa-Bunko. This village, located near the large naval base of Yokosuka on the road to Yokohama, has an interesting history. It has the second oldest library in Japan, founded in the thirteenth century by Sanetoki Hojo who was the grandson of a regent of the Kamakura military government or shogunate. The library was rebuilt in 1930 on the spot where it had always been, and it has many priceless books as well as a few important statues. Kanazawa-Bunko is no longer a village community today. It is filled with modern tract houses and has become a large suburb of Yokohama, completely blending with the westward extension of the huge Tokyo urban sprawl.

"There is no time in Japan quite like the New Year, which is the greatest and longest holiday of the nation, lasting at least three and often five days. All business is suspended except for essential services, and friendliness is the keynote of the season. Innumerable people call on each other, often only leaving a calling card. Millions of cards with season's greetings are also sent by mail, as in the West." Cities and resorts are crowded. So are theaters, parks, shrines and temples. Banquets and feasts are held everywhere.[20]

Family and friends gather for festivities and specially prepared foods of great traditional importance. *Mochi* (rice cakes) and *zoni* (*mochi* with vegetable broth) are imperative at New Year's festivities, as rice has always been a sacred food in Japan.

20

It is customary to observe sunrise and to celebrate the first bath on New Year's Day. Many games are organized for children. Houses are decorated usually with a pair of pine trees (for long life) at the entrance, and three bamboo stems (for constancy and virtue) in back of each tree.[21] A twisted rope (*shimenawa*) with hanging white paper strips (*gohei*) is strung across the top of the entrance. These are ancient Shinto customs: The rope is sacred and keeps out darkness, as it kept out evil when the Sun Goddess hid in her cave in Shinto mythology.[6] The white paper streamers are symbolic of an offering of cloth to the Shinto altar dur-

ing worship [*see text in Chapter III*]. "Added to the house decorations can usually be found fern leaves (for expanding good fortune); an orange (because its Japanese pronunciation "daidai" also can mean "from generation to generation"); and lastly a lobster (whose curved back suggests old age and thus longevity)".[20]

PANEL 10   "For years the child is strapped to his mother's back, sharing in a half-drowsy state her warmth and her rhythm . . . feeling sheltered and close to the maternal body, which means to him life, protection, company and goodness . . . The unconditional surrender of the adult Japanese to the rhythm of fate, his apparent contentment in being buffeted by the great forces beyond his control and his horror of isolation, could well have been molded on the traces left in his unconscious by those securely fettered and lovingly balanced states of early childhood".[11]

An everyday scene in the past, the mother carrying her child on her back is still seen frequently in suburbs, small towns and the countryside. At left is a woman securing her child on her back with the help of a sister or friend in the gardens of Engakuji Temple in Kamakura. It is one of the five great Zen temples of Kamakura built in the thirteenth century after Southern Sung priests imported Zen Buddhism from China. The women above, seen in Kanazawa-Bunko [*see text in Chapter IV*], has a much older child strapped to her back; she also carries another one in front of her in a special seat behind the handlebar of her bicycle, as often occurs in Japan today. The principle of constant closeness to the mother remains the same. (Both pictures were taken in 1987.)

23

PANEL II

It is frequent in Japan, as in many countries in the West, for a family to go out for lunch on Sundays. This may or may not be in the course of a day's outing. The picture above shows an entire family out to lunch at Kogo restaurant in Arashiyama which is a favorite excursion spot near Kyoto, popular since Heian times. Here generations of tourists and families and lovers have emulated the habits of the Heian nobility and sought pleasure in floating down the River Oi in long wooden boats in an exceptionally beautiful natural setting.

The young girl on the right is also in Arashiyama. She is dressed in a beautiful kimono with the usual large sash and an elaborate, ornate hairdo. This shows that many women, young or old, —even in cities—can still be seen in traditional Japanese dress when they go out for a special occasion. The girl is in a doorway close to her mother (not shown) and gave me her consent for this picture. (Both photographs were taken on Easter Sunday 1987, not a holiday in Japan.)

24

PANEL 12   Schoolgirls of all ages seen everywhere are delightful for
their gentleness, their spontaneity, their sweet innocence.
This has been repeatedly observed ever since I first came to
Japan in 1954, and it is still true today [PANEL 13R]. These
four junior high schoolgirls were photographed in 1985
on the grounds of Kyomizu-dera, another famous temple
in Kyoto. This temple is dedicated to the Eleven-faced-
Kannon, a foremost Buddhist deity. Established in 885,
it was rebuilt after a fire in 1633 by the third Tokogawa
shogun.

This photograph (1981) shows a group of high school girls on Shijo Street near the Gion Shrine, also in Kyoto. They are startled by the sudden photograph. Older girls are more restrained than their younger schoolmates, but are just as sweet and gentle. One of them makes the Churchill "V" sign with both hands as a greeting, or as an expression of glee [*see text*, PANEL 4].

PANEL 13   Japanese mythology embodies three concepts: Deities (or *kami*), Nature and Man. They are intimately related in the Shinto tradition in which man appears "not as a creation of God, but as a child of the *kami*". Thus human nature "remains innocent and does not emerge from the Garden of Eden corrupt and radically evil".[6]

The innocent radiance of Japanese children is apparent in these two photographs. The picture here shows a little schoolboy and a Japanese variety of basketball played in a Kyoto schoolyard in 1981.

28

Above is a group of radiant young girls in 1987 on a junior high school excursion to celebrated Mt. Hiei (*Hiesan*), where Japanese Buddhism grew out of the teachings of an almost legendary ninth century priest named Saicho. The girls spontaneously surrounded Mrs. Watkins-Josselyn who told them a story in Japanese. She is the Japan-born daughter and granddaughter of protestant missionaries, co-founders of Kyoto's famed Doshiha University which is now a very large private teaching institution.

 WOMEN

MUCH HAS BEEN WRITTEN about Japanese women, but very few authors have perceived the essence of Japanese femininity as well as Lafcadio Hearn, an American author who lived and wrote in Japan in the nineteenth century. Many of his observations are quite relevant today. Hearn believed that "the spiritualization of women" so dear to the Occident was one of the greatest blocks to an understanding between East and West. This ideal, fostered by centuries of influences from the Greek idea of classical beauty to the exaltations of chivalry and the Renaissance, does not exist in the Orient.[16] In effect, the chivalric idea that man "should not only protect, but also compliment, divert and please women, in short court them, separately from physical desire . . ."[17] is incomprehensible to the Far Eastern mind. So is the pervasive "sentimental exaltation of love" in Western literature, not "because it treats of love per se, but because it implies virtuous maidens, and therefore the family circle." The Japanese has no objections to passion or infatuation based on physical attraction, but he believes that it is not that sort of love which leads to the founding of a family.[16] This double moral standard, accepted in the Orient, has always been frowned upon by the more puritanical Western societies and has remained an essential difference between the two.

A mixed society where "the supreme refined charm" is that of women has never existed in the Far East. Even today, despite appearances to the contrary in some cosmopolitan circles where business men and their wives mingle with foreigners, Japan has remained essentially a man's country. In addition, "public display of affection" towards anyone has long been considered improper. "After babyhood, there is no more hugging and kissing," is a rule which holds for all classes of society. In effect, "Japanese affection is not uttered in words, it is chiefly shown in acts of exquisite courtesy and kindness."[16]

With such a background, what then is the true position of Japanese women? Foreigners have scant if any knowledge of this. As often happens in Japan, logic does not apply and what is apparent defies what is real. The nation's oldest archives indicate that Japanese women held a most important place from the very beginning of organized life on these islands, long before

recorded history. Many women are venerated in the Shinto pantheon, and "early female divinities are at least as numerous as male ones. The source of all life and light, the eternal sun, is a goddess, fair Amaterasu-o-Mikami," the oldest and most important deity in Japan. Women "serve the ancient Gods" in famous shrines, [PANELS 16L,38L,42] and appear in all Shinto pageants."[16] The "natural rights" of women have never been opposed by Shinto nor later Buddhist influences. On the contrary, women have been worshipped extensively in both religions. While the "lives of holy women hold honored place in Buddhism, . . . in a thousand Shinto shrines throughout the land, the memory of woman as wife and mother is worshipped equally with the memory of man as hero and father."[16] Feminine leadership was common in the third century and there were ruling empresses as late as the eighth century.[5] In the Heian period, Fujiwara court ladies were unequalled in literature and the arts. Finally, in the home Japanese women have long held the dominant role over husband, children and all household affairs, a role they have retained to the present time [PANEL 84].

Early Confucian principles reinforced by centuries of Tokugawa feudal rule firmly established the social system of arranged marriages and of double standard within the Japanese family: For women, no social life outside of home and family; for men, relative freedom to do as they please. In addition, the pressures exerted on Japanese men by their very special "techniques of interpersonal relationship" result in both excessive nervous fatigue and emotional exhaustion. This may explain in part why they seem to have such a great need for bars. There are more bars in the back streets of large cities' shopping centers than in any other country [PANELS 88–90].[10] Both Reischauer and Nakane give good descriptions of these small, dimly lit and elegantly cozy bars where men gather with a few friends after work to drink and talk and unwind: "Here the bar hostess, successor to the geisha tradition, engage them in amusing and . . . titillating conversation. This can lead to more serious relations and for some bar girls to a more prosperous life as a mistress or even a wife . . . The milieu may be different, but the spirit of the modern Japanese bar is close to that of the amusement center of feudal times."[5] The few remaining geishas concentrated in the geisha houses of large cities are Japan's classic entertainers. They are not prostitutes but have been trained since childhood to develop exquisite grace, manners and competence in conversation, dance, song and musical instruments [PANELS 85–87]. Regrettably, they have just become too expensive for the average businessman.

Modern women, however, are changing "in spite of their generally subservient position in the broader society." They no longer walk behind their husbands, who are often the ones carrying both bundles and babies [PANEL 58]. Not only do they run the household, but often pamper their husbands and take all paychecks giving only a small allowance in return. Japanese women are now well educated. They all have twelve years of schooling, but relatively few go on to college. They are usually expected to marry by age twenty-six, so they are unlikely to stay in the job market for more than a few years after school, professional women excepted. These are fewer than in the West, but there are many women doctors.[5] Women have retained their legendary prominence in literature and the fine arts, and they have become successful in creative occupations such as fashion, design, publishing, advertising, and others. Since 1947 women have had "full equality with men, yet few women can be found in politics." By and large, Japanese women do not have the Western attitude about the sinfulness of sex. To them, it has always been a natural phenomenon which is to be enjoyed in its proper place.[1] With the advent of AIDS, this will probably change. When all is said and done, however, "most women fall back into the fold" after marriage. Marriages tend to be stable, perhaps because of "the wage discrimination against older divorced women in the labor market, and the difficulty for them to remarry."[5]

Reischauer gives an excellent discussion of the reasons why the Women's Liberation Movement has not gathered much momentum in Japan: "Women in recent decades have made such huge advances that they are still busy digesting them . . . In spite of much lower wages for women, new opportunities have given them much greater economic independence since World War II . . . They now frequently have a social life of their own outside the family [PANEL 21]. But maybe more important

is that the 'women's lib' movement simply does not fit their style."[5] While Japanese women will continue to change in the future, most of them are still "proud of their dominant family role" and do not feel driven to change it. Neither do they feel compelled to reject or neglect home and children in favor of a career. They seem to combine both rather well. In fact, it is unlikely that the core of Japanese life would be remodelled on the pattern of Western society, for this might involve the "dissolution of the family and the breaking up of traditional life" to a far greater extent than has already occurred in Japan.[16] Enough social disintegration has taken place in the post-war years, so that few Japanese, especially women, would really wish for more.

Rather, it is likely that the immemorial qualities of devotion and selfless attachment to home and family of Japanese women may prevail. Indeed these traits have been inbred for so long as to become innate, inherited from "ages and ages of unquestioning faith." Given the right circumstances, these qualities usually reappear. So does the "conception of life as duty, a touching gratitude for every small kindness, and childlike piety" with love for all living things.[16] More important perhaps is the delightful feminine smile, which can also "embrace the senses with a gentle affection" rarely felt elsewhere. I believe with Malraux[15] that love in Japan is not a conflict and much less a contest, but "the trusting contemplation of a loved one, the incarnation of the most serene music, a poignant tenderness." On the whole, Japanese women have been under less rigid constraints than men, and therefore could remain more natural, perhaps closer to the nirvana of childhood alluded to in the previous chapter. Thus, the radiance and innocence of children, hidden in the collective Japanese unconsciousness, is much closer to the surface in women than in men. Consequently, women in Japan may exhibit this inner radiance interwoven with various shades of beauty not only in their smile, but in a serene, gentle, almost ephemeral aura, often apparent until late in life [PANELS 12,17,19,23–26,29,30].

It is still a part of the basic pattern of Japanese life to take a newborn child to a local shrine to present him to the Shinto gods (*kami*), usually around the 20th day of the baby's life. This brief ceremony (*omiyamaeri*) takes place irrespective of the family's religion, for everyone in Japan—except for the most forbidding Christians—also follows Shinto customs [*see introduction to Chapter III*]. The photo on the left shows a grandmother holding the newborn child with obvious delight as the beaming mother reaches towards it. Sometimes the family prefers to bring the child to a famous shrine, as is the case in this picture

taken in April 1988 at the Grand Shrines of Ise. These are the most ancient and sacred sanctuaries in all of Japan. One of these is dedicated to the goddess of food and crops, the other to the Sun Goddess herself, the most revered deity in the nation.

The picture above is taken on a sunny holiday afternoon in May 1988, and shows a mother and daughter having a late luncheon at a pleasant small riverside restaurant in Arashiyama. This is situated in a beautiful natural setting by the River Oi and has been a well known excursion spot near Kyoto for almost a thousand years [*see text, Chapter IV*].

The picture on the left shows two young actresses on a village set at the TOEI movie studios in Uzumasa, a Kyoto suburb. Both girls wear dresses of the Edo period; the one on the left portrays a young dancer (*odoriko*), the one on the right an apprentice geisha (*maikosan*). The history and literature of Japan reach back over so many centuries that they furnish an endless stream of stories and tales, both legendary and real, for stage and screen plays. Cloak and dagger warrior (samurai) stories of the Edo period are particularly abundant, like American Westerns.

The two young kimono-clad girls above were attending a large party at Arashiyama [*see text Chapter IV and* PANEL 14] and gracefully posed for this picture. (Both photographs taken in 1987.)

PANEL 15

PANEL 16   There are many women in Japan who have retained a natural grace that is truly captivating. As important perhaps, is the delightful feminine smile "which can embrace the senses with a gentle affection" rarely felt elsewhere [*see also* PANEL 19].[16] Most attractive Japanese women do not convey the sense of sexual overkill frequently seen in the West. Their general preference is to please and complete a man, not to compete with him.

On the left is a girl selling tickets near the stage of an open-air special dancehall at a Shinto shrine in Kyoto (1987). On certain days and at given times, sacred dances or *kagura* are performed by Shrine maidens called *miko* [PANEL 42]. These dances bring to mind primal Shinto rites of purification. Since ancient times, women have held an important position in Japanese life and have always been venerated in the Shinto pantheon. Above is the wife of the owner of Kimpei, a moderately priced but excellent restaurant in Yokohama. This attractive lady is seen behind the counter of her place, bent over a dish which she is preparing with the utmost care (1987).

PANEL 17   The naturalness and spontaneity of young women in Japan is a constant source of amazement and delight to most foreigners. Above, the smiling salesgirl in a Kyoto perfume shop appears overcome with joy, as if given a wonderful present.

This bemused and tranquil girl is a waitress in a Kyoto restaurant which serves only Japanese crepes prepared in many different ways. She is waiting for orders in a private dining room. Guests are seated at a low table on floor mats (tatamis).

PANEL 18   Both photos show young people, either college students or early in their working lives. Here again, there is pervading gentleness and good humor but no rowdiness or rough edges.

The group above is seen on the temple grounds of Chio-in Kyoto (1985). This temple is the Grand Headquarters of the Jodo sect founded in 1211 by Honen, a celebrated Buddhist priest. His effigy, carved by himself, can be found behind the main assembly "Hall of the Thousand Mats". Chio-in is one of the largest and most famous temples not only in Kyoto but in the whole country. The temple's two storied gate (Sammon), 80 feet high, is considered the most imposing of temple gates in Japan. Also on an eminence in the temple grounds is "a famous belfry with the largest bell in all Japan cast in 1633, and rung during an entire week beginninig April 19, while there is a daily service in commemoration of Honen".[20]

The photo on the right shows two young people jesting in front of a crowd waiting for a bus in Arashiyama [*see text*, PANEL 14].

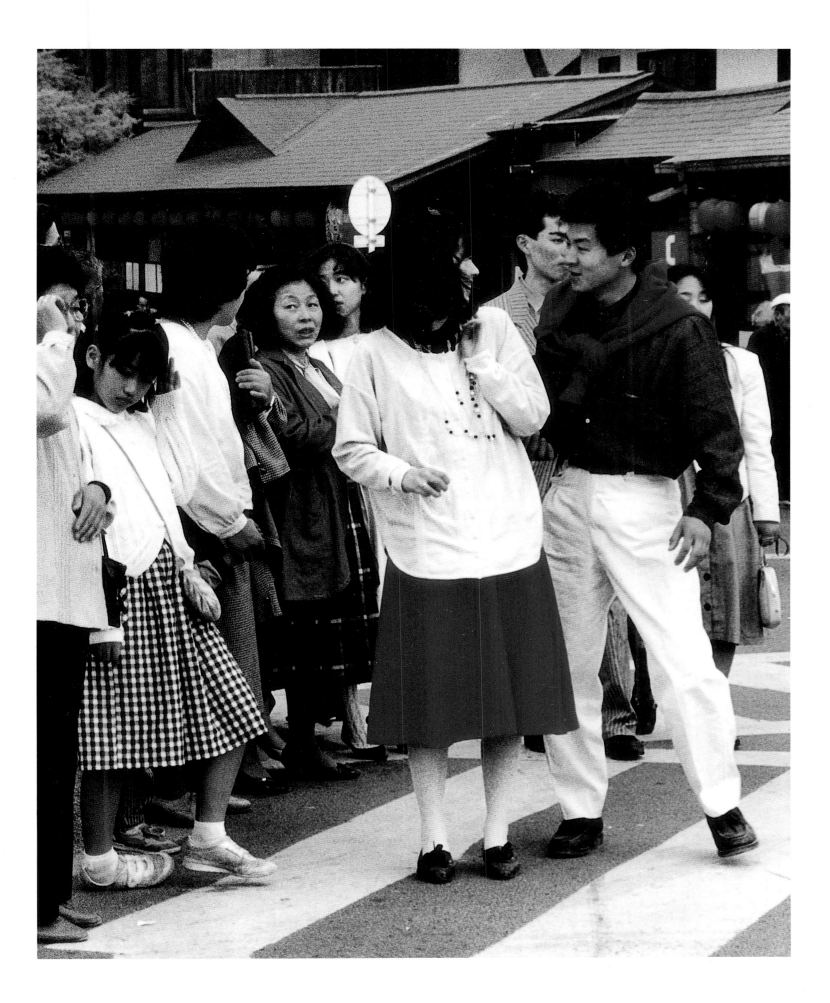

Many coffee houses now dot the main streets of Japanese cities. It is a pleasant experience to sit and watch the world go by in those small, aesthetically designed, very modern places, most of which serve delicious pastries.

Both photographs (1987) show the wonderfully natural and soft expression of these young women. They incarnate the very essence of the Japanese feminine in youth, in contrast to the ladies in PANEL 25R, who are classic examples of the Japanese feminine in adulthood.

PANEL 19

PANEL 20 Girlguides leading groups of students or tourists can be seen all year throughout the length and breadth of Japan. Above is a guide leading a group of schoolchildren over the Uji Bridge on the grounds of the grand Shrines of Ise. These most ancient and sacred of Japanese sanctuaries are located four miles apart in a grandiose cypress park near Toba, two hours by train south of Kyoto. There is the Gekku, or outer shrine, dedicated to the goddess of farms, foods and crops, Tokouke-no-Mikami; and there is also the Naiku or inner Shrine dedicated to the Sun Goddess, Amaterasu-o-Mikami, "primal ancestor of the Imperial line and the most revered deity in all Japan".

The symbols of imperialdom are the mirror, the jewel and the sword. The mirror is in the inner sanctum of the Naiku, the sword is at Nagoya's Atsuta Shrine and the necklace at Tokyo's Imperial Palace. The inner sanctum at Ise is surrounded by four fences. Only the emperor or his delegates can proceed beyond the second fence, usually on New Year's Day. Both shrines are demolished and entirely rebuilt on adjacent areas every twenty years as a symbol of purification through renewal. This process has been going on for 1,200 years and will probably continue for all time to come.

On the right, the girlguide leading a sightseeing tour at Horyuji in Nara [*see text*, PANEL 34R] is particularly cheerful; many of her colleagues show signs of "burnout", as the work is repetitive and exhausting.

46

PANEL 21   The postwar affluent society and technological progress in household appliances have freed women from much domestic drudgery and have given them much greater economic independence. Modern women are changing "in spite of their generally subservient position in Japanese society. Now they all have twelve years of schooling, but still few of them go on to university training. Junior colleges often fill the role of 'finishing schools' as most girls look forward to having home and children". Except for high school, about half of all the school teachers are women. They have found acceptance both in the professions and in creative occupations. But in general, it is still true that "jobs available to girls after school are less prominent than those offered to men".[5]

Women now often have a social life of their own, and they may go out alone or in groups, not only to tearooms but also to restaurants or other events, just as men do. They usually wear Western clothes, but they may still be seen in traditional Japanese dress [PANELS 15R, 25]. Both pictures were taken in 1987 and show groups of women having lunch at Kanazawa-en, an old Kanazawa-Bunko inn which was a Japanese Navy officer's club during World War II. Kanazawa-Bunko is close to the huge naval base of Yokosuka, which is still the headquarters of the U.S. Navy's Seventh Fleet.

49

PANEL 22 While Japanese women "will continue to change in the future, most of them are still proud of their dominant family role" and they do not feel driven to change it.[5] The social experimentation of the sixties which has raised such havoc in the West has not spared Japan entirely. However, thanks to remarkable group adaptability, things have settled to an acceptable pattern not wholly dissimilar from long established custom. Women do not feel compelled to reject home and children in favor of a career. A few seem to combine both rather well, considering this is at best extremely difficult.

In fact, it is unlikely that the core of Japanese life would be remodelled on the pattern of Western societies, for this might involve the "dissolution of the family and the breaking up of traditional life" to a far greater extent than has already occurred in Japan.[16]

Both photographs were taken in 1981 in Momoyama-minami-guchi (Peach Hill-South-Exit), a residential suburb of Kyoto [*see text*, PANEL 7].

PANEL 23 In general, Japanese women are under less constraints than men, and therefore can remain more natural, perhaps closer to the Nirvana of childhood alluded to in Chapter I. Thus, the radiance and innocence of children, hidden in the collective Japanese unconsciousness, is much closer to the surface in women than in men. As a result, women in Japan may exhibit that inner radiance interwoven with various shades of beauty not only in their smile, but in a serene, gentle, almost ephemeral aura, often apparent until late in life [PANELS 24L, 26R].

The girl above is seen at Sanzen-ji, an ancient Buddhist temple with magnificent gardens. It was founded in the eighth century at Ohara, a farming village near Kyoto, by a remarkable priest, Saicho, who imported the Tendai sect from China and started the liberalization of Buddhism in Japan.

The group at the right is pictured sightseeing at the Todai-ji, one of the original seven great temples of Nara, dedicated to the newly imported sects of Chinese Buddhism between the sixth and eighth centuries [*see text*, PANEL 6].

Since ancient times, a fair has been held the twenty-fifth of every month at the Kitano Shrine in Kyoto [*see text,* PANEL 71]. This fair gives the visitor a wonderful opportunity to catch a few glimpses of the Japan of long ago and to see many different types of Japanese men and women (1987).

The mature lady in Japanese dress seen on the left still has great beauty and poise. The two aged women pictured above bending over a shopping bag, exhibit a certain pastoral closeness people shared in homogeneous societies of premodern times.

PANEL 24

PANEL 25   Both pictures are taken in 1987 at the Gion district's theater in Kyoto, before a performance of the colorful Miyako Odori. This is an annual dance show given by the Gion geisha, starting on April 1 and running for six weeks [*see text* PANELS 85, 87 *and Chapter VI*].

The pleasant and natural women above dressed up in their lovely kimonos and chatting over the show's program form an interesting contrast to the more pensive and elegant group shown on the right.

宝 戒 寺

建武2年(1335年)足利尊氏が北条一族の冥福を祈るため寺地を寄
進し,開山は惠鎮で,開基は後醍醐天皇です.本尊は地蔵菩薩で三茶仏師
憲円が貞治4年(1365年)に作ったもので重要文化財です.

Hokaiji Temple

In 1335 the Shogun Ashikaga Takauji contributed this land to
build the temple to pray for the repose of the souls of the Hojo
clan and this temple was founded by Emperor Godaigo.

The principal image of this teple is "Jizo Bosatsu"

(an important Cultural Treasure) made in 1365 by the

Buddhist-image-carver Ken-en.

世界人類が平和でありますように

PANEL 26 The Kamakura region is one of the most important in Japanese history. It was the site of the first military government in Japan set up in 1192 by Minamoto Yorimoto, the first shogun (supreme military commander). It was also in Kamakura that Zen Buddhism first came to Japan from China in the twelfth century. Kamakura abounds in ancient crafts, such as armor, swords, ceramics, lacquerware, and most of all sculpture. Except for a busy small downtown section filled with art and craft shops, the Kamakura area has remained a large and varied natural park, dotted with impressive ancient temples, both Shinto and Buddhist. The extraordinary temple grounds and nearby areas are always harboring a local life that is rich and vibrant, yet composed and gentle [PANEL 60L].

This splendid old lady, seen at the ticket window of the Hokaiji Temple in Kamakura, has the warm expression of one who had joy and love and sorrow in life, and is now contented. A brief notice on the history of the temple can be read on the signpost to the left. (Both pictures were taken in 1987.)

PANEL 27 According to ancient custom, women retainers from time to time come on the grounds of the Imperial Palace in the center of Tokyo and tend the gardens for free, out of devotion and respect for the Emperor and his family. This unusual photograph was made possible by Dr. Fuji, a Japanese physician who spent a year's training in Medicine with us at the Yokosuka U.S. Naval Hospital. Dr. Fuji belonged to a prominent Japanese family who had permission to keep their horses on the Imperial grounds. In the fall of 1955, he graciously invited all the doctors in the Department of Medicine at the Naval Hospital to visit the Imperial Grounds and to see a horse show in which his father was participating. Thus, I had the rare experience to walk through parts of the Imperial grounds and to witness the scene shown here.

A similar voluntary and devotional tending of the grounds takes place in other sacred enclosures in Japan. The photo shows two women—one of them a Red Cross worker—weeding the path around one of the temples on Mt. Hiei (Hiesan), a sacred mountain near Kyoto where the eighth century Japanese priest Saicho (Dengyo Daishi) founded a monastery to propagate the teachings of the Tendai sect. Mt. Hiei remained a leading center of Japanese Buddhism until the sixteenth century; because the monks had become too powerful and troublesome, the monasteries and all their buildings were scorched to the ground by Oda Nobunaga. All structures destroyed in 1571 were rebuilt in 1980.

PANEL 28 The New Year's celebration in Japan is the nation's most important holiday. Women dress in beautiful kimonos, and everyone visits friends, family, shrines, theaters, spas and other resorts [*see text*, PANEL 9]. Above are two ladies in traditional dress passing in front of the gate to the Shomyogi Temple on New Year's Day 1956 in Kanazawa-Bunko, at that time a small seaside village. The second oldest library in Japan was founded there in the thirteenth century by a relative of a Hojo regent of the Kamakura shogunate.

This library is situated by an oval pond in the enclosed garden of the small Shomyogi Temple, which has taken care of the books and treasures since 1333, when it lost contact with the Hojo family. The library was rebuilt in 1930 on the spot where it had always been. Besides books, documents, and some priceless early Buddhist statues, it has a complete set of sutras published in Sung China in the fifth century (*from a leaflet of the Temple*).

The two conversing ladies on the right were photographed in 1955 at Ama-no-Hashidate, "famous from ancient times for its beautiful views, which make it one of the Scenic Trio in Japan", the other two scenic spots being Matsushima Island off the coast of Sendai in the north, and Miyajima, in the Inland Sea near Hiroshima.

Ama-no-Hashidate is situated near Myazu Bay facing the Sea of Japan, four hours NW of Kyoto. The name means literally "Bridge of Heaven" and is taken from the mythological and sacred "Floating Bridge of Heaven" on which Izanagi and Izanani stood while they created the Islands of Japan. "Actually it is a sandbar across a small bay. This sandbar is two miles long and some two hundred feet wide on which are groves of pine trees bent into fantastic shapes by wintry storms".[20] The best view is obtained from Monju Hill, where this photo was taken. It does not show the sandbar as it focused on the more interesting ladies, but the Bay crossed by the famous sandbar is seen in the background.

PANEL 29 The relaxed, peaceful woman shown here is selling Japanese sweets and the region's special pickled vegetables at her sidewalk stall in the farm village of Ohara, on the outskirts of Kyoto [*see text, Chapter IV and* PANELS 65–68]. She wears the special costume of her village, and the label *Ohara Me* (or Ohara Woman) is printed on the collar of her kimono, woven out of a heavy material known as *katsuri* (1987).

The old lady at right seen at the forefront is trying to buy a train ticket from a ticket vending machine at the small station of Kita-Kamakura. In spite of her advanced age, this lady is quite noticeable for her soft features and for her completely natural demeanor. She has the gentle and dignified bearing seen in older Japanese women, and perhaps more so in the countryside.

Ticket vending machines are ubiquitous in Japanese train stations, but these machines can only be used by persons who can read Japanese. Foreigners must go to a special section with English speaking employees available in larger stations. In small stations, they can try their luck with the employee behind the only window. If this fails, they will manage to buy their ticket from the train conductor.

Both photographs of these wonderful Kyoto women were taken in May 1988, and demonstrate that the unique radiance so particular to many Japanese women still exists today.

The photo on the left shows a girl in her early twenties working in a tearoom and wrapping up a package of Japanese delicacies. The tearoom itself is in a house of classic Sukiya design at the edge of the old and elegant Kodaiji district, in the foothills of Higashiyama in Kyoto.

The elegant woman in the green blouse was seen walking her little dog in the gardens of the temple of Kennin-ji, situated between the ancient Gion and Miyagawacho geisha districts. She is probably in her late forties and has the great softness of women who have long endured both good and bad without becoming bitter, as they have tempered their expectations and learned to take life as it comes without the harsh madness of those who want it all.

Kennin-ji Temple has particularly beautiful and serene grounds. It was founded in 1202 by the celebrated priest Eisai who brought Zen to Japan from China. Of the original buildings, only the extraordinary two-storied middle gate remains just beyond the curved stone path on the far right of the above photo. This gate was the residence of a famous warrior of the Taira Clan, whose long conflict for power with the Minamotos became the subject of a legendary medieval tale.

PANEL 30

 CUSTOMS

CUSTOMS FLOW from tradition which is anchored in the bedrock of history and sometimes goes back to the wellspring of legend. In the Preface, we mentioned that the Japanese character is fashioned early in life by three sets of cultural influences: Shinto, Confucian and Buddhist. The same is true for Japanese tradition which is particularly rich in Shinto folklore. A mere outline of Japanese customs would fill many books, therefore only those aspects of traditional life which convey the gentle or touching note of the familiar will be considered here. Flower arranging and the tea ceremony may first come to mind, but the elegant arrangement of a few flowers and twigs in an understated display is like brush painting, "a simple expression of the essential." [18] Similarly, the tea ceremony's original meaning is "to look quietly into oneself and appreciate nature within a rustic teahouse" while green tea is being served with grace and beauty. [19] Thus, flower arranging and the tea arts may draw from Shinto's love of nature and purity, but they are more properly viewed as classical disciplines of Zen Aesthetics and do not fall within the scope of *Gentle Ways*.

Shinto, or the Way of the Gods, is Japan's native and primitive cult, based on the love of nature and ancestor worship. It is an integral part of life and is indelibly imprinted in the social fabric of the nation. This has been so since the very beginning of the Japanese people. At the outset, it taught the intrinsic goodness of the human heart. [20] As Nature in Japan is "beautiful and bountiful," the ancient Japanese came to believe that all that is beautiful is good and pure [PANELS 5R,40,65L,68,69]. Similarly, they felt reverence for any object or places in nature which inspired them with a sense of awe or wonder or even the divine. Such places or objects then became deified as *kami*, or divine spirits—gods with a small "g." In effect a *kami* may be anything above the measure of Man. There are *kami* in Nature, such as a stone, or tree, or a typhoon. "There are *kami* of the family, clan, village, nation. But the most venerated, the dearest of gods are the dead. The spirit of ancestors, which governs the realm of the living, is perceived to be everywhere, in the rhythm of the seasons, in the weather, in fortune, good or bad." In fact, the

dead are invited back each year at the midsummer festival of Obon (a Shinto analogue of All Souls' Day) to participate in the summer dances. [21,22]

Some 100,000 shrines throughout Japan assure the survival of Shinto as the "structure of beliefs and ideas upon which the basic pattern of Japanese life is built." Thus, a shrine is a "sacred area on which buildings or some votive marker are erected to enshrine the *kami* worshipped there" [PANELS 33,45,70,71]. [22] The Shinto calendar "gives modern life its framework," because the year is punctuated by shrine festivals which celebrate important agricultural or national events [PANELS 40,45]. [6,22] As a reflection of the way of life of the ancient Japanese, Shinto rites and tenets are essentially simple. Worship consists of bowing humbly for a minute or two, followed by an offering of food or drink, and a prayer. Formerly, cloth was added as an offering. It has now been replaced by strips of white paper (*gohei*) hanging in clusters from a rope [PANEL 33] or from a twig of the sakaki tree [PANEL 36] as a symbol for cloth. [20] Shinto beholds only the good, which is pure. It does not recognize evil, only the impure such as decay or death. Thus, purification is essential before any act of worship, and can be achieved in one of three ways: By "waving a wand of paper streamers symbolically over the person or place to be purified (*harai*) [PANEL 36]; by washing either in the sea, a river, or under a waterfall (*misogi*) or by rinsing hands and mouth at a shrine fountain [PANELS 34,35]; by avoidance of certain words or actions (*imi*). For example, never use the work "cut" at a wedding; do not attend any celebration when in mourning because of impurity; avoid "four" in numbering floors in buildings or elevators because the number 4 and the word death are both pronounced "shi" in Japanese, and so on. [22]

In contrast with Western religions, Shinto has no founder, no book, no dogmas, and up to the sixth century when Buddhism came with Chinese civilization, no name. [22] For Bellesort [12] it was "the most accommodating of all religions," and for Reischauer, it "expressed an attitude of joyful acceptance of life . . . where life and death were seen as part of the normal process of nature . . . The only concern was with ritual

70

purity . . . which contributed certainly to the Japanese love of bathing and their record of being undoubtedly the world's cleanest people throughout history."[23]

Curiously enough, no religion or government has ever succeeded in displacing Shinto as "the local religion of agricultural communities and the supra local cult of the nation."[22] Shinto came to a friendly agreement with the overwhelming forces of Buddhism brought by China in the sixth century, and created a "double aspect Shinto" (Ryobu) where most *kami* could be viewed as manifestations of Buddhist deities. Yet, in the long run Ryobu vanished and Shinto prevailed unchanged.[20] The protracted attempts at conversion by Christian missionaries since the fifteenth century remained finally without major effect. The Meiji "modernizers" of Japan and the pre-World War II "imperial expansionists" tried to turn Shinto into a militaristic state religion. This too failed, and "Shinto reverted to what it has always been, an unassuming but powerful flow of the natural order which permeates all of Japanese Life."[22,23] Perhaps Shinto's penchant for perpetual renewal together with its "gentle feeling for life and nature"[6] have allowed it to coexist with other religions and philosophies without ever being submerged. Perhaps Shinto has also given the Japanese people the magic key to adapt as well as they have to fifteen centuries of social and political upheaval, but particularly to the industrial and technological worlds which they have so rapidly mastered.

A perception of *Shinto mythology* is also helpful in understanding some current Japanese customs and beliefs. Picken, in his classic text on Shinto[6] explains that the "Ancient Japanese, while perhaps poor in material culture, were rich in many kinds of spiritual awareness . . . They learned to commune with the Universe they inhabited. The tradition of Shinto has continued to express this for them ever since, and underlies their culture and life." There were no holy texts before the *Kojiki* (or Record of Ancient Matters) was compiled at the end of the seventh century, when the Japanese learned to write with Chinese characters. Up to then, "Shinto mythology had been preserved only by oral tradition and the perpetuation of rituals."[22] It is in the *Kokiji* that legend was first written down as history.

According to the mythology of creation, "the universe became gradually defined through the work of a great many *kami*—or gods—united in pairs representing opposite extremes." For Picken, the idea of unity or balancing equalled that of harmony.[22] This might well be the genesis of the harmony necessary to reach group consensus, a concept so dear to the Japanese. After a long succession of *kami*, the "inviting male" Izanagi and the "inviting female" Izanami were born. They became in time the progenitors of the Sun Goddess. "While standing on the Bridge of Heaven, they threw a jeweled spear into the sea and created the first Japanese Island on which they descended. They learned how to make love by watching birds and they engendered many more islands and *kamis*." The last of these was the *kami* of fire which burned Izanami to death. Overtaken with grief, Izanagi "follows her to the underworld where he is ordered not to look at her. He disobeys and sees her decomposing remains covered with maggots."[22] The ugly keepers of the netherworld threaten "to kill one thousand people every day should Izanagi ever return." He claims in turn that he "can cause fifteen hundred people to be born daily. This is taken as an affirmation of the power of life over death, a strong theme in Shinto thought."[22]

Izanagi then goes to a river (perhaps the river Isuzu near the present Ise Shrines, or the river Tachibana) and washes himself completely to get rid of all impurities. "Herein lies the Shinto concept of purification through water (*misogi*)" [PANELS 34,35]. As Izanagi washes his face, he gives mythical birth to "the three final *kami*; the *kami* of the stars, the *kami* of the moon and the primal *kami* of the sun, Amaterasu-o-Mikami."[22] The Sun Goddess is very important to the Japanese, as she is considered to have given rise to the first Emperor, and thus to the Imperial Family in an uninterrupted line down to the present time. In 1945, the Emperor Hirohito publicly renounced any claim to divinity, but customs die hard and legends remain encrusted in the collective psyche probably forever.

An old Shinto symbol seen everywhere in Japan is the twisted rope (*shimenawa*) hung over a door, or near the entrance of a shrine or temple [PANEL 33]. The purpose of this rope, very ancient in origin, is to keep out impurities or darkness (by inference evil). Legend tells us that Susano-no-Mikoto, *kami* of the stars and brother of the Sun Goddess, "was given to wild behavior and committed acts of impurity that would offend the other *kamis*."[22] For example, he would "break down the ridges between rice fields and fill up irrigation ditches, type of offenses formerly viewed as criminal, and purified in later ages by the rite of *obarae*.[6] The Sun Goddess, Amaterasu, outraged at her brother's "disruptive behavior," retreated in the Heavenly Rock Cave and plunged the world in darkness. The other *kami* attempted to lure her out of the cave by laughing and making noises while Ame-no-Uzume performed a revealing and lascivious dance.[24] When at last Amaterasu came out, probably driven by curiosity, the waiting *kami* "quickly threw a rope over the entrance of the cave to stop her returning and the world again had light."[22] Susano is expelled by the other *kami*. "The triumphal world of Japan then begins with the liberation of Izumo—the most sacred of national shrines—from the clutches of a huge dragon, and the descent on earth of Amaterasu's grandson, Nigini-no-Mikoto, the first imperial ancestor."[21]

A great many *Japanese customs* are therefore firmly rooted in Shinto tradition and Shinto legend. Just as shrine festivals punctuate the Shinto calendar with important seasonal events, so is a person's existence marked by progressive stages. In Shinto, this flow of life is like the flow of water "pure, clear and plentiful." An important point here is that change is connected with renewal, not decay."[6] Shortly after birth, a Japanese baby is taken to the local shrine to offer thanks to the *kami* [PANEL 31]. At ages three, five and seven, the visit is repeated [PANEL 32L], and again at twenty with "the coming of age." Marriage is a Shinto ceremonial [32R]—even for Buddhists—, which is often followed by a Western style reception, usually quite expensive. As life's horizons narrow, "there are shrines and temples which help people prepare for a peaceful death." Yet Shinto, which forever reaffirms brightness and purity, is concerned mostly with life rather than death. How-

ever, when death comes the Japanese usually defer to Buddhism [PANEL 54]. As the departed one becomes an ancestral *kami* to be revered on the *kami* shelf (*kamidana*) formerly present in every home, his memory will also be enshrined in the family Buddhist altar (*butsudan*).[6]

While the twisted rope over the door or near the entrance suggests the predominance of brightness over darkness (or life over death) by "keeping out" impurity, many other facets of daily life do the same. The meticulous cleanliness of sushi-bars [PANEL 36L], for instance, is "an expression of the Shinto ideals of purity and beauty," as is the aesthetic design of many houses, store fronts and everyday objects [PANELS 76, 92R]. Similarly, the removal of shoes before entering any dwelling or place of worship—whether Shinto shrine or Buddhist temple—literally keeps out dirt [PANEL 49]. By the same token, suspended white paper strips (*gohei*) or sakaki branches and piles of salt at the entryway of any house, temple or shrine [PANEL 33] invariably bring to mind the ancient rites of purification[6] as do sacred dances performed at the larger Shinto shrines [PANELS 42,16L].

Popular beliefs also maintain a good number of customs. Fertility rites known since antiquity are still performed today in some parts of Japan "at the time of transplanting rice seedlings into the paddies." By using genital symbols these rites represent an "attempt to employ human sexual fertility to insure abundant crops."[24] The carp is a symbol of virility, and Boy's Day is observed late in April throughout rural Japan by flying as many carp-shaped banners on one's roof as there are boys in the house [PANEL 44]. A twig of pine suspended at the door on New Year's Day "invites the gods to protect home and household." The Festival of the Stars on July 7 (Tanabata) commemorates ancient purification rites just one month before the very popular dances of Obon when the dead return to earth and everyone rejoices. Obon is Japan's most important holiday after the New Year. Good fortune and good luck charms are for sale in all larger Shinto shrines [PANEL 38], and in former times were available almost at every street corner.[21] Perhaps most important, is the ubiquitous *torii* or entrance gate to any Shinto shrine, be it only a grove of trees or a special waterfall. The origin of the *torii* is uncertain. Coming perhaps from India via China, its trademark is the "rectangular cut of its uppermost beam." The curvilinear shape of that beam came from China only in the sixth century, as did the *torii*'s bright vermillon color [PANELS 5R,6R,37–39L, 81L]. Before then, in its pure ancient Shinto form, the uppermost beam was almost straight and the tint was that of natural wood [PANEL 43L]. Legend has it that a *torii* represents the perch on which the rooster crowed to lure the Sun Goddess Amaterasu out of her cave![21]

Food and its presentation are exceedingly important in Japan, and assume almost the character of a ritual. Rice certainly has such significance, as there is both a goddess (Uga-no-Mitama) and a famous shrine (Inari, in Kyoto) for this sacramental food [PANELS 87–88]. The Fox is the earthly messenger of the goddess of rice, and there still are thousands of smaller Inari shrines throughout Japan [PANEL 39L]. Food-related customs still abound: One must not plant chopsticks into a bowl of rice, for it is thus that offerings are made to the dead. Fresh fish also holds special ritual value, as in ancient times it was brought in offering to the Shinto altar. While the usual meals consist of rice and fish with pickled vegetables and the inevitable soya sauce, there are innumerable specialty restaurants. Some serve only one type of food: sushi (raw fish on rice) [PANEL 36], regional specialties, tempura [PANEL 76R], noodles, sukiyaki, eel, Japanese crepes [PANEL 79], and so on. Others are classified along price lines, from popular places where available dishes are shown in plastic in the window [PANEL 78L], to medium priced ones with counter or table service on the ground floor and private rooms uptairs [PANEL 46], to very fine restaurants where all service is in elegant private rooms and meals are exhorbitantly expensive [PANELS 47,80]. The exquisite and always aesthetic presentation of dishes, even in medium priced establishments, is unequalled in any other country [PANEL 48].

There are also many customs of Buddhist origin which permeate daily life. For example, Jizo is the popular god of children; small, smiling, with a shaved head, usually shown in sculpture with brightly colored bib and hat [PANEL 69R]. Remembrance of Jizo consists in placing stones in front of him for the souls of small children in the netherworld.[21] Daruma, on the other hand, is a "good luck charm in the shape of a rotund legless doll. Daruma is a contraction of Bodhidharma, the legendary Indian patriarch who brought Zen to China and sat facing a wall for nine years, thus losing the use of his legs."[9] Anyone making a wish may buy a Daruma. Upon making the wish, black ink is applied to one eye. If the wish comes true, the other eye is colored in.[9,21] Thus, a politician running for office invariably places a large Daruma with one eye colored in at the polling place [PANEL 50L]. Lastly, many Gentle Ways can be found in Buddhist temples. Some of these quaint customs are borrowed from Shinto, such as temple fountains [PANEL 34R] and bells to wake up the slumbering god [PANEL 51R]. Some others are purely Buddhist in origin, such as temple calligraphers sitting in the entrance ticket booth, and who—for a small fee—will validate one's presence at a given temple in beautiful script with impressive stamps entered in special booklets some visitors carry to that effect [PANEL 52R]. In addition, there are bronze incense burners of varying sizes at all Buddhist sanctuaries. The burning of incense at these temples is an expression of hope for spirituality as well as a votive offering to the dead [PANEL 53].

Many Japanese customs are firmly rooted in Shinto tradition and in Shinto legend. Just as shrine festivals punctuate the Shinto calendar with important seasonal events, so is a person's existence marked by progressive stages. In Shinto, change is connected with renewal, not decay.[6] So then are the various rites of passage in the flow of life. Shortly after birth a Japanese baby is taken to the community shrine to offer thanks to the local god (*kami*).

On the left, a mother in lovely kimono holding her three week old infant wrapped in gorgeous traditional silk, stands on the Uji Bridge over the sacred river Isuzu. She is seen returning from the Ise Shrine, the most important shrine in all Japan, after having presented her child to the gods of Ise, or maybe even to the Sun Goddess Amaterasu-o-Mikami, the most venerated deity in the land. The same theme—already mentioned in the chapter on Women because of the extraordinary expression of the mother and daughter shown in PANEL 14—is repeated here because of its age-old, yet perennial recurrence. The happy young mother and her child, suggest a timeless entity inseparable

from surrounding Nature, and incarnating not only rebirth and renewal, but also the serene essence of eternal Japan (April 1988).

Above, the same ceremony (*omiyamairi*) is taking place in an ordinary country shrine in presence of the local Shinto priest, but the intent is the same. On the very first visit of the baby to a shrine about 20 days after birth, the father and other male relatives are usually absent. In recent times however, men have started to come along, but they still stay in the background. (*This photograph is reproduced with permission from both Fine Photo Agency, Tokyo and Picken.*[6])

PANEL 32   At ages three (*san*), five (*go*), and seven (*hichi*) the child's visit to the shrine is repeated to ask for the *kami's* continued protection. This now takes place in a ceremony for many children of different ages and their families (Hichi-go-san). The event could be remotely compared to a first communion in three stages, two years apart. (*This photograph is reproduced with kind permission from Meiji Jingu, Tokyo.*)

Above is a wedding. In Japan, this is always a Shinto ceremony, even for Buddhists. It is often followed by a Western style reception, usually quite expensive. The Shinto ceremony itself can also be very onerous because of rental of costly wedding kimonos. In addition, custom demands that for every gift received (usually an envelope with cash), a gift be given in return. To reduce expenses, some young couples follow the example of a few prominent Japanese who avoid all the fuss by flying to Hawaii for a church wedding and a few days of honeymoon at much less cost.

PANEL 33
In ancient times, offerings at a Shinto worship consisted of food, rice wine (sake) or a piece of cloth. The cloth has long since been symbolically replaced by strips of white paper (*gohei*) hanging in cluster from a rope, as in these photos, or from a twig of the sakaki tree (a sacred ever-green)[6] [PANEL 36R].

A twisted rope (*shimenawa*) hung over a doorway or near the entrance is also a Shinto symbol seen everywhere in Japan. It is of interest that the twisted rope can also be seen at the entrance of a Buddhist temple as shown on the right over a side door of the Nigatsudo, an early temple of the Nara period founded in 752. The purpose of this rope is to keep out impurities or darkness, thus fostering life over death (or evil, which Shinto does not recognize). In legendary times, the Shinto gods (*kami*) who had been trying to lure the Sun Goddess Amaterasu out of a dark cave where she had hidden in protest over the outrages committed by her brother, "quickly threw a rope over the entrance of the cave when she finally came out, and the world again had light".[22]

Shinto is a most accommodating religion and soon came to a friendly agreement with the overwhelming forces of Buddhism brought in from China in the sixth century: Most Shinto gods could be viewed as manifestations of Buddhist Deities and many Shinto customs became Buddhist ones.

78

PANEL 34 Shinto beholds only the good, which is pure. It does not recognize evil, only the impure such as death or decay.[6] Thus purification is essential before any act of worship and can be achieved in one of three ways: By washing in the sea, a river or under a waterfall [*this page*]; by rinsing hands and mouth at a shrine fountain [*page 81*]; or by waving a wand of paper streamers symbolically over the person to be purified [PANEL 36R].[6]

This photo shows the more demanding purification by standing under a waterfall (*misogi*). (*It is reproduced with permission from both Haga Hideo, Tokyo and Picken.*[6])

The photo on page 81 shows high school girls about to rinse their mouths at a fountain before entering Horyuji, "the oldest existing temple in Japan and perhaps the most antique wooden structure in the world". This was reportedly the first Buddhist temple in Nara, and was dedicated in 607 by Prince Shotoku, the founding father of the Japanese state.[20] The simple purification rite at a fountain standing on the grounds of a Buddhist temple is another example of a Shinto custom having been integrated into Japanese Buddhism.

PANEL 35   The Kitano Shrine in Kyoto is an ancient and well known
Shinto sanctuary founded in the tenth century [*see text in
Chapter V*]. This photo shows an impressive two-story
gate, the Romon, built in 1892. A tablet hung beneath the
eaves bears the verse "Forefather of Learning, Master of
Poetry" transcribed from an illustrated scroll of stories
about the origin of the Shrine, calligraphed by a twelfth
century Fujiwara master. To the west is a plum tree garden, wonderful in the spring. To the East is a grove of pine
trees where Hideyoshi held a famous grand tea ceremony
party in 1587 (*from a current Shrine leaflet*).

82

Shown here is the simple act of purification by rinsing hands and mouth before worship at the shrine [*see introductory text*]. Shinto worship is essentially simple. It consists of bowing humbly for an instant or two in front of the main shrine after having rung the bell to wake up the *kami*, followed by tossing a coin in the wooden hopper and a short prayer.

PANEL 36 The central concern of Shinto with renewal through ritual
purification is manifested in many ways, one of which is
the spotless and brightly polished sushi-bar.[6] The one
shown here is in Kyoto's Fujita Hotel. Another example is
the Japanese's love of daily hot baths (*ofuro*) "which makes
them undoubtedly the world's cleanest people".[23]

Above is purification (*oharai*) by waving a wand or a twig of the sacred sakaki tree to which white paper clusters are attached over the place or persons to be purified.[6] In this case, the purification ceremony is conducted by a Shinto priest at a small altar in the new Los Angeles office of a Tokyo firm, to invoke the help of the gods (*kami*) for prosperity and good luck in the new business venture.

86

Both pictures (1988) show the Inari Shrine, twenty minutes from Kyoto on the Keihan line. It is one of the most famous Shinto shrines in Japan. It was founded in 711 and dedicated to the goddess of rice and food, Uga-no-Mitama, plus several other deities.[20] The gods worshipped here "are regarded as the fundamental ancestral deities who protect the necessities of human life, clothing, food and housing. There are more than 10 million worshippers, high and low, rich and poor, who visit this shrine every year, and who attend its many festivals".

The imposing entrance gate [*left*] is guarded on either side by large stone figures of the fox, believed to be the sacred earthly messenger of the goddess of rice. "The bushy tail of the fox symbolizes fruitful years of rice, and the key held in its mouth symbolizes the key to the rice granary". The other fox on the right (not shown) holds a precious stone in its mouth to symbolize the spirit of the deities enshrined here (*from a leaflet of the Shrine*).

The above picture shows a small "votive tablet shrine" (*ema-do*) located in the wooded hills beyond the large inner worship hall of the Main Shrine. The *ema-do* is an integral part of larger Shinto sanctuaries and combines very well the religious and superstitious sides of the Japanese character. A simple Shinto altar is bedecked in white cloth and a few symbolic offerings under the sacred twisted rope (*shimenawa*) with hanging white paper streamers (*gohei*)—the very hallmarks of Shinto [*see text*, PANEL 33]. The woman, bowed in a brief prayer, evokes how deeply committed most Japanese are to the Shinto belief. Conversely, the neat rows of hanging votive tablets (*ema*) behind the table on which to write one's wishes and prayers to be hung with the others in the shrine, are a most touching aspect of Shinto primitivism which rightly enough asks for the gods' help in life's many problems. The two wooden hexagonal good fortune boxes on a small table at the right of the picture are present in every shrine, and remind one of Shinto's ancestral superstitions.

PANEL 38 During the feudal age, Kyoto's Inari Shrine at Fushimi was given the first grade of court rank and early in the Meiji period (1871) it was raised to the rank of "Taisha", the highest status among national shrines. Over the centuries, members of the Imperial family, feudal lords and warriors made substantial offerings by dedicating shrine buildings and providing for ever costly repairs. The custom of giving tangible goods to the Shrine has spread to people at large, who over the years have given numerous *torii* gates, shown here in both pictures.

These *torii*—donated by faithful worshippers in prayer for thanksgiving and happiness—have been placed one next to the other to form long corridors which spread for several miles in the grounds and wooded hills behind the shrine, and which—under various shades of sunshine—make for splendid color effects. Each *torii* given to Inari-san (a popular name for the Shrine) has been lacquered in vermillion to symbolize peace and good harvest. In addition to individuals, many businesses are giving *torii* to the Shrine in gratitude for success or in hope of prosperity.

Both pictures were taken at the Uesugi Shrine in Yonezawa, Yamagata prefecture. Now a silk-weaving center in the north of Japan near Fukushima, this medium sized city was once the castle town of the Uesugi family which ruled the fief for almost three centuries during the entire Edo period. Uesugi Kenshin became the most powerful lord of his clan at age thirteen after having served in a monastery and studied military science in Kyoto. "In 1551, at age 21 after having been made Governor General of the Kanto, he was adopted in the Uesugi family. At 22, he adopted the Buddhist name of Kenshin, became a priest, and the Uesugi Shrine was dedicated to him".[20]

Above stands an Inari Shrine with multiple red *torii* near the entrance of the Uesugi Shrine in Yonezawa's Matsugasaki Park. Throughout Japan, some 30,000 Inari shrines—usually close to another Shinto shrine—are dedicated to the goddess of rice and food, Uga-no-Mitima. As in Kyoto's original Fushimi Inari Shrine, the red *torii* are given by faithful worshippers in "thanksgiving for happiness, prosperity and mutual respect" or in the hope of further success. Stone figures of the fox—the earthly messenger of the goddess of rice—seen in every Inari shrine, are also gifts from its believers.[20]

90

The Japanese, who more than any other modern people are attuned with Nature, believe it "provides through its well marked seasons the framework for the flow of life". By the same token, at various important stages of life, the Japanese revert to the ancient Shinto custom of "calling on their protective gods (*kami*) to invoke their help. This is done often by offering or writing prayers on the back of wooden prayer tablets (*ema*) which are then hung on trees or on specially sheltered boards". These requests are often sad and moving. One lonely man asks for help in "finding a nice home-loving girl to marry". Another is by a mother praying for "better fortune in a life saddened by a handicapped child".[9] The wooden prayer tablets are quite different from the multitude of paperstrips found hanging on tree branches near good fortune boxes at some Shinto shrines. These strips contain predictions found wanting by people who drew them from the box and who then hung them on tree branches hoping that the local shrine gods would turn a bad fortune into a good one.

PANEL 40   The Heian Shrine in Kyoto is a famous Shinto sanctuary
dedicated to Emperor Kammu in 1895 "to commemorate
the 1,100th anniversary of the founding of the city. Located
in Okazaki Park, the buildings are colored in bright vermillon with blue tiles on the roof and are a replica of the
first Imperial Palace built in Kyoto in 794. There are two
festivals a year, one on April 15, and another much more
important on October 22nd. This is called the Jidai Matsuri and features a procession marching through the city
composed of groups dressed to represent important epochs
in the history of Kyoto".[20] The gardens at the rear of the
shrine (shown here in 1956) are famous for their cherry
blossoms in the early spring and their iris in May.

92

This photograph was taken in Tokyo. Cherry blossom
viewing (*ohanami*) has been a celebrated custom in Japan
for centuries and has been a favorite subject for generations of famous painters of screens, panels and scrolls.
"Weather forecasts in the spring always include minute details of the dates on which blossoms are to appear, and
enormous traffic jams develop at popular viewing places
where people are seeking a glimpse of the blossoms and a
place to eat, drink and sing".[6] (*Reproduced with permissions
from both Photo International Agency, Tokyo and Picken.*[6])

PANEL 41 Shown here is a display of decorative lanterns in the lobby of the Fujita Hotel in Kyoto at the time of the April 1987 Miyako Cherry Dances in the Gion geisha district [*see text in Chapter V*].

On the right is a special cart featured in Kyoto's ancient Gion Festival in Kyoto, held since 876. Very early in the Heian Period, "when a plague swept the country, the head priest of the Yasaka Shrine, popularly known as the Gion Shrine, assembled a large procession with highly decorated festival carts to seek of the protection of the gods against the ravages of the epidemic." The festival lasts for two weeks starting July 10th. On July 17 and 20, "a procession of gorgeous floats passes through the streets of the city. The floats are of two kinds: the *yama* carried on the shoulders of a great many men, and containing one or several figures artistically displayed; and the *hoko*, a kind of ornamental tower on massive wheels which is also splendidly decorated. There is usually a mast in the center of the tower about 120 feet in height".[20] The Naginata Hoko is one of these carts with a long sword or spear attached to the top of its mast, and is shown waiting for the procession in a narrow side street in 1962. Many of the old carts represent the "highest developed art of doll making, weaving, embroidering, dyeing, carving, painting and lacquer".[26]

"The ceremony begins with washing of the floats which is performed at Shijo Bridge, where a presiding priest dips a branch of the sacred sakaki tree into Kamo River and sprinkles it symbolically over the Shrine. The next day a boy in beautiful costume rides to the Shrine to receive the rank of sacred page (*chigo*), a very high but costly honor. This page will dance on a *hoko* on the 17th, and join the procession that same day and on the 20th. On the evening of July 16th, the floats are being lit by paper lanterns (*chochin*) and brilliantly prepared. Each house also displays a lantern or two, and its anteroom—glowing with antique folding screens—is open to public view".[20] During the processions on the 17th and the 20th *hokos* and *yamas* are accompanied by mounted knights clad in ancient armor, priests and "bearers of the divine spear, shield, bows, arrows and swords". The festival is concluded on the 28th by another ceremony of washing of the floats, similar to the first.[20]

PANEL 42 Japanese women have held a most important position "almost from the very beginning of organized life on these islands". Many women are venerated in the Shinto pantheon, and "early female divinities are at least as numerous as male ones. The source of all life and light, the eternal sun, is a goddess—fair Amaterasau-o-Mikami", the most important deity in Japan. Women serve the ancient gods in famous shrines and appear in all Shinto pageants".[16] The sacred dances (*kagura*) performed at the larger Shinto shrines and shown here at the Inari Shrine in 1988 [*above*] and at the Kitano Tenjin in 1987 [*right*] both in Kyoto,

bring to mind the ancient rites of purification.[6] The *kagura* are usually performed in special halls set apart for this purpose. These halls have a raised platform of several feet and are open on three sides so that the dances are plainly visible to those standing around. The sacred dance shown above was requested by a lady sitting at the far right of the stage but not shown in the picture.

96

"The dances are performed by shrine maidens called
miko, clad in white vestments with long divided red skirts".
But for the red color, these girls would be reminiscent of
white-robed vestal virgins in the temples of ancient Rome.
Dances are sometimes scheduled for the public but more
often performed on request by buying tickets from a girl
sitting at a low table near the stage [PANEL 16L]. "Each
miko holds in her hand a branch of the sacred sakaki tree, a
fan or a number of tiny bells [*left*]. The orchestra consists
of the flute, clappers, Japanese harp (*koto*), small wood-
wind instruments and a drum".[20,21] Above, a *mikosan* serves
sake at the end of a performance (1987). This is symbolic of
an offering during Shinto worship [*see introductory text*].

PANEL 43 Good fortune and good luck charms were formerly available almost "at every streetcorner".[21] Good luck charms can now be bought at the larger Shinto shrines. Above is a stand where those *omamori* and other souvenirs are for sale at the Ise Shrine, the most celebrated in Japan because it is dedicated to the Sun Goddess, the founding deity of the Imperial line [*see text and* PANEL 43].

The young girl [*left*] in white blouse and red long skirt is a *mikosan,* or traditional helper in Shinto shrines. The good fortune box (*omikuji*) is displayed close to the entrance of a Shinto sanctuary in Sendai [*above*] the most important city in northeast Japan. Sendai was largely rebuilt after World War II. (Both photos were taken in 1985.)

PANEL 44 Boys' Day is a national holiday in Japan, held annually on May 5.

The carp is a symbol of fertility in Japan and for several weeks preceding Boys' Day, as many carp-shaped banners are flown on one's roof as there are boys in the house. This custom has remained most prevalent in rural areas, but the flying carps are seen in towns and cities as well and even on ships in port. The picture above is taken in Ohara, a small farming village northeast of Kyoto (1987).

Starting in late April, a splendid ancient panoply is often displayed in the home's main alcove [*tokonoma*] as a symbol of militarism and as a reminder of past glory. The picture on the right is taken in the hallway of a Kyoto restaurant in 1987.

PANEL 45   The most important holiday in the Japanese calendar is the New Year's festivities which last three days, during which everything closes except for vital services. After days of preparation of special foods for feasts and parties [*see text of* PANEL 9] everyone dresses up [*left*] and goes visiting friends and relatives. Shrines as well as theaters, restaurants, and resorts are filled to capacity. For many Japanese, the New Year celebrations and the summer holiday of Obon, (when the dead are welcomed back on earth with special dances) are the only vacations taken, even if they are entitled to three weeks or longer.

These are two ladies in traditional Japanese dress and hairdo on New Year's Day in 1956. The photo is taken in a square of the seaside village of Kanazawa-Bunko [*see text, Chapter IV*].

Vast throngs are seen on their way to the Hachiman
Shrine in Kamakura, also on New Year's Day 1956. It is
estimated that during the three day holiday more than a
million people visit this shrine which is a major Shinto
sanctuary dedicated to the God of War.[6] While a visit to a
Shinto shrine is a must on New Year's Day, it should be
noted that on New Year's Eve every bell in all Buddhist
temples throughout Japan is rung 108 times, as a reminder
of the year's end forgiveness of Man's 108 sins!

PANEL 46 Both photographs show Kimpei restaurant in Yokohama
in 1987. This is a reasonably priced establishment with excellent and varied food [*see introductory text*]. In such
places, however, no one speaks English and the name signs
and menu are always in Chinese ideographs (*kanji*). Thus,
foreigners have a difficult time finding them and ordering
the right things, unless taken there by a Japanese.

104

On the left, the entrance to Kimpei is not devoid of aesthetic appeal. Above, guests dine sitting on tatamis at low tables as shown, or at the counter, from which this picture is taken. Shoes are always removed when sitting on a tatami floor, but may be kept when eating at the counter. There are also several private dining rooms upstairs where the fare is always more costly.

PANEL 47 More expensive restaurants all have individual rooms for private dining. Such rooms are usually designed in the streamlined and aesthetic Sukiya style. It derives from a unique tearoom architecture developed in the sixteenth century by Sen-no-Rikyu, "the greatest teamaster of all time". This is the elegant alcove (*tokonoma*) of a private dining room at Osaka's Kaminabe restaurant (1981). It features special dishes wrapped in paper and cooked at the table on a small charcoal brazier. Because of a special coating, which is a secret of the house, the paper wrap does not catch fire!

106

Here, the waitress bowing at the entrance of Tokyo's Egawa restaurant (1985) performs the very Japanese custom of saying goodbye with grace and politeness. Little rock gardens with a few green plants (as shown) often have a small fountain with a stone lantern. These miniature gardens bring into innumerable homes and public places the Zen concept of understatement and the message that Buddha is "immanent in all things".[9] One or two waitresses will often accompany departing guests into the street and walk with them a short while before a last deep bow and goodbye.

PANEL 48 Food and its presentation are exceedingly important in Japan and assume almost the character of a ritual. Rice certainly has such significance, as there is a god for this sacred food which has been brought in offering to the Shinto altar since the beginning of agrarian life in these islands, more than two thousand years ago [*see introductory text*].

The aesthetic presentation of food in a great variety of simple but elegant dishes is observed in the simplest places. However, such displays become exquisite in the better restaurants, and attain rare beauty and refinement in the most expensive ones. On the left, a *sashimi* (raw fish) plate at Kimpei in Yokohama (1987) [*see* PANEL 46]. Above, a tablesetting with hors d'oeuvres awaiting a dinner party at Higashiyama Villa in 1985. This is a stately mountain retreat converted into a luxurious restaurant in the hills of Kyoto.

PANEL 49 Another example of the ancient Shinto concern with "renewal through purity" is the removal of one's shoes before entering any house or place of worship. Shoes are usually left in the entrance of any house, outside a private dining room if in a restaurant, or on special shelves in the case of temples, shrines or some museums. Slippers of all sizes are always available everywhere near the entrance. They must be worn to walk along the corridors and hallways of any dwelling or public place, but must be removed and left at the door before entering any tatami-covered room. Shoes are left outside a private dining room in an Osaka restaurant (1981) and arranged in neat rows by a waitress or other employee.

Here is a large group of schoolchildren looking for their shoes after a visit of the Byodo-in, a serenely beautiful Fu- jiwara villa converted into an Amida Buddhist temple in the twelfth century. At that time, in reaction to the asceti- cism of early Chinese and Tendai Buddhism, there emerged among the late Heian court nobles a wish for "an easier road to enlightment and the cult of Amidism was the simplest yet devised. It involved walking around an image of Amida Buddha while continually chanting his name".[9] The belief that one could pass away with ease and peace gave rise to beautiful Amida halls with lovely ponds (a part of it can be seen in background of photo) to give the im- pression of earthly paradise. Such halls "could double as a villa, and could serve ultimately as a mausoleum".[9]

PANEL 50   There are also many customs of Buddhist origin in Japanese daily life. The big roly-poly doll sitting in a polling place in Kanazawa-Bunko, a suburb of Yokohama, is a good luck charm, called Daruma, a contraction for Bodhidharma, a legendary Indian patriarch [*see introductory text*]. Anyone making a wish may buy a Daruma. On making the wish, black ink is applied to one eye. If the wish comes true, the other eye is colored in.[9] Thus, a politician running for office will always place a large Daruma in the polling place (1987).

Since early childhood every Japanese has a love of singing. A frequent custom following any dinner party
(whether celebrating a festive occasion or not) is to sing.
Books of lyrics for well known songs are available at many
restaurants [*above*], as well as at many snack-bars which are
open until four in the morning. Accompanying tapes with
full orchestration (*karaoke*) can also be played on good re-
corders so that amateurs may enjoy themselves trying to
perform like professional singers. In some restaurants,
waitresses will sing to entertain guests or join in with them
as at Egawa in Tokyo (1985). In a few private homes, the
owners have built a sound-proof music room in the basement to sing at any time without disturbing the neighbors.

PANEL 51   This is a man who sits in the ticket booth at the entrance of the Kennin-ji in Kyoto collecting admission fees and giving information about the temple. He is also a calligrapher and the Keeper of the Seals for that temple and is writing a few beautifully penned Chinese ideograms on the goodness of Buddha or some other religious theme in a special book that visitors collecting such inscriptions carry with them. The small entry fee is usually different for each visitor. The various seals of the temple are then affixed in vermillion ink, making for a striking effect. The stone ink-ing pad with a slight depression at one end for water (*suzuri*) and some brushes are seen beyond the calligraphers' right hand. Ink painting, used in China for thousands of years, came to Japan in the seventh century. The Kennin-ji is a remarkable temple founded in 1202 by the priest Eisai who first brought Zen from China [PANEL 30]. Except for the Middle Gate, every structure was re-built in the eighteenth century. There are some 15 subordinate temples on the grounds. Eisai is buried in one of them.[20]

The photograph shows a woman praying in front of a Buddhist temple in a quiet courtyard off Teramachi, a busy covered shopping lane in the center of downtown Kyoto. This is a Jodo temple, a major Buddhist sect founded in Japan in the twelfth century by the celebrated priest Honen, who taught that salvation lies in the all-saving powers of Amida Buddha. The ceaseless repetition of the formula "Glory to Amida Buddha" (*Namu-Amida-Butsu*) "is considered merely an expression of a thankful heart".[20] The long rope to ring a bell high under the temple's eaves is pulled to awaken the slumbering Buddha. This is one more example of a primitive Shinto custom adopted by Buddhism centuries ago. The photo emphasizes again the deeply religious feeling of the Japanese people, who defer to Buddha and to Shinto gods on a daily basis, as a way of life, rather than in a scheduled weekly service in a temple or shrine.

PANEL 52

Buddha's original theme in fifth century B.C. India, was the pessimistic belief that life was unending suffering with a perpetual cycle of birth, death and rebirth. Release from this cycle could take thousands of lifetimes. Buddha's Great Enlightenment revealed that this painful cycle could be broken only by giving up desire, the source of all pain. He taught that by following the Eightfold Path, a highly moral code, one could—with the help of meditation— reach enlightenment or Nirvana, the "blissful state of extinction of all desire". The Eightfold Path has made Buddhism a universal religion of "gentleness, peace, compassion and moral grandeur".[9,20]

Buddha's unmodified strict teachings (Hinayana or "smaller vehicle" Buddhism) go on today mostly in Sri Lanka, Thailand and a few other isolated Southeast Asian pockets. On the other hand, "greater vehicle" (Mahayana) Buddhism that migrated to China in the first century A.D. was highly adaptable and blended well with Chinese civilization. The pragmatic Chinese in the first century A.D., as

would the optimistic Japanese five hundred years later, rejected from Buddhism all that was properly Hindu: metaphysical dreams, the cult of inertia, terrors of the Gods, ecstatic stupors, bodily injury.[9] In Nara Japan, Buddhism blended successfully with much of Shinto. Other significant Japanese innovations consisted in searching for easier and more practical ways to reach enlightenment, and thus Nirvana. These various ways, broadly speaking, define the beliefs of the many Buddhist sects alive in Japan today. On the whole, Japanese Buddhist priests are pleasant, tolerant and compassionate. They exhibit little if any of the forbidding sectarianism so often manifest in Western and Mideastern religions which have tried to follow in the footsteps of Moses, Jesus, or Mohammed.

The smiling priest above was photographed in 1981 at Byodo-in, an eleventh century splendid Fujiwara villa which later became the focus of Amidism, "the simplest road to enlightenment yet devised". Amidism involved nothing more than walking around an image of the Amida Buddha

116

while chanting his name. This aristocratic cult is now extinct but gave rise to Jodo and Jodoshin, two popular variations of Amidism and two of the largest four contemporary Buddhist sects; the other two are Nichiren and Zen. In Zen, salvation may come through immediate and instantaneous enlightenment by pursuing "mental and physical discipline, simplicity and frugality. Look carefully within and there you will find the Buddha".[20] Perhaps the Zen priest above reflects these qualities. The photo was taken in 1987 at the Saihoji, a remote Kyoto temple, famous for its moss gardens and a fourteenth century Zen "rock waterfall".

117

PANEL 53   The Todai-ji is the largest and probably oldest wooden structure in the world (built in 752) and one of the few remaining original seven Buddhist temples in Nara. It houses the Great Buddha of Nara, the largest bronze statue known anywhere [*see text,* PANEL 6]. The vast temple grounds are always swarming with visitors, as the Great Buddha is a unique sight and a virtual must for children and adults alike [PANELS 6L, 25R]. It is surely equal to the Seven Wonders of the Ancient Hellenic world.

Both photos show a very large incense burner at the entrance of the monumental hall, the Daibutsuden. The burning of incense at a Buddhist temple is an expression of hope for spirituality as well as a votive offering to the dead. (The photo at left was taken in 1955, the one above in 1987.)

PANEL 54 The Japanese way of death is a curious blend of Buddhist ritual, Gentle Ways and universal mortuary practice. Cremation is the rule, except for members of the Imperial family, dignitaries and people in remote parts of the country. When someone dies at home, the family contacts the mortuary; arrangements are then made for appropriate decorations, visits by friends and relatives, and finally cremation, all to take place the next day.

The outside of this house is bedecked with white and black cloth. A small white tent is erected in the street by the entrance for later visitors to sign a register and leave an envelope with a modest sum in cash. Each visitor will later receive a small gift from the family. Inside the house, close to the entryway, an altar is set up over the coffin with white drapes and white flowers. In the center hangs a large black framed photograph of the deceased plainly visible from the front door. In later life, most Japanese keep such a picture at home in anticipation of death.

Except for Christians, all Japanese whether Buddhist or Shinto, reach Buddhahood at death and are given a new name by the attending priest in keeping with the Buddhist belief of perpetual rebirth. This new Buddhist name is cal-ligraphed on a white tablet placed by the coffin. In front, are beautiful flowers and offerings. At a set time the following day, relatives and friends come to pay their last respects. Each visitor steps in the entrance but not in the room, makes a short bow as he puts three pinches of incense in an incense burner on a small low table, and leaves after a short silent prayer. When the last visitor has gone, the coffin is removed for cremation and close family can then be entertained and stay overnight. The ashes are returned the same evening in an urn which is placed in the home altar (*butsudan*) and will be given a Buddhist burial later in the family plot.

120

The white tablet bearing the deceased's new Buddhist name is then replaced with a black lacquer one inscribed in gold which will stand forever in the *butsudan*. This is "the place in a Japanese home where the ancestors of the household are enshrined, fed, tended and revered by the living. There is often in the same room a *kamidana* or shelf for the Shinto *kami*, which exists to protect the home, the community or the locality".[9] When death occurs away from home or in a hospital, the body is cremated on the same day and the ashes are sent to the family. The customary funeral is then held at home or in a Buddhist temple. A temple service may also take place after a home funeral or if a large crowd is expected. In such cases, there is always a catered reception afterwards.

The photograph at the left was taken in 1981 in Momoyama-minami-guchi, a suburb of Kyoto. Above is the abbotts's cemetery at the temple of Chio-in in 1985. This is the headquarters of the Jodo Buddhist sect, the most prominent in Japan. A long succession of illustrious abbotts are buried there. The cemetery is in a beautiful setting near the present abbott's residence, high in the woods above the temple grounds in Kyoto.

IV COUNTRY LIFE

T HE MOST PERSISTENT, and some of the most valuable features of the Japanese people, even in our own day, are legacies of rural life."[11] We have seen in the Preface that the persistence of old, traditional structures in Japan made most city people think like the Japanese of long ago.[1,10] Japanese life has for centuries depended closely on what grows in the soil or comes from the sea, and on limits set by nature upon small organic communities with age-old customs framed by the rhythm of the seasons. For Singer, the Japanese—symbolically at least—"have never been torn from the familiar circle of animals, flowers and rocks." The dominant cause for Japan's legendary durability, is that "in the minutest details of daily life, it has followed those hints of Nature which Western nations have too often disregarded."[11] For these reasons and because Japan is an essentially non-urban nation in spite of its large cities, it is in a rural setting and in the villages that the foreigner will best "begin to savor the remarkable coziness and peculiar charm of the flow of ordinary Japanese life."[11] Thus, Gentle Ways as familiar aspects of existence may be more readily apparent in the countryside than in large towns and cities.

Most of the photos in this chapter focus on four localities: **Kanazawa-Bunko**, a seaside village on Tokyo Bay in 1955, now a vast suburb of Yokohama; environs of **Kamakura**, some eight miles from Kanazawa-Bunko, and the site of the first military government (shogunate), in 1192; **Arashiyama**, a beautiful riverside spot, thirty minutes drive from Kyoto and first chosen for excursions by twelfth century Heian emperors; **Ohara** and vicinity, a unique mountain village in the Northeast outskirts of Kyoto, also well known since Heian times. In addition, glimpses will be seen of Koshiba, a fishing village near Kanazawa-Bunko [PANEL 64], tea-culture in Okayama's Korakuen Park, and Miyajima Island off the coast of Hiroshima [PANEL 57].

History does not usually have a causal relationship with the familiar, except in those instances where—in a given setting—a particular event or pattern becomes a custom, then a tradition and finally a quaint facet of daily or seasonal life. This sequence of events, however, has happened in both Arashiyama and Ohara. In the former, the natural setting of pines and cherry trees transplanted from Yoshino is so compelling that gen-erations of lovers and families and tourists have emulated the excursion habits of the Heian nobility and sought pleasure in floating down the River Oi in long wooden boats. The waters are crowded with visitors not only at cherry-blossom time and in the fall with its gorgeous cascades of red maple leaves, but pretty much all year long. The long wooden boats of Arashiyama are reminiscent of gondolas in Venice. In both places, a traditional custom has become a gentle aspect of the familiar [PANELS 58R, 59].

The same is true for Ohara, where the historical background is richer and more varied. Ohara is a serene and bucolic valley near the lower slopes of Mount Hiei. A famous monastery now stands near the top, first founded by a most remarkable eighth century Japanese priest, Dengyo Daichi, or Saicho. He profoundly changed the evolution of Nara Buddhism by introducing the Tendai sect from China in the early Heian period. The school of Buddhism that Saicho established on Mt. Hiei lasted for several centuries. He was the first to free early Japanese Buddhism from the "cloying liturgy and endless metaphysical disputation that was throttling Nara Buddhism."[9] Tendai is only a small sect today, but two of its earliest temples still exit in Ohara. Saicho dedicated the most important of the two, the Sanzen-in, in the late eighth century, and since then the chief abbotts have all been members of the Imperial or noble families. They left many artistic treasures among which is the Main Hall, originally built in 985.

The other temple, the Jakko-in, is both smaller and older [PANEL 68]. Built on a wooded slope in an exquisitely beautiful setting, it conveys to a high degree the Buddhist concept of life's impermanence, perhaps because of its history. It was first dedicated in A.D. 594 by Prince Shotoku himself (the founding father of the Japanese State in the Asuka period), and it later became a Tendai temple. The well known twelfth century *Tales of Heike* is an epic saga of two illustrious clans, the Minamoto and Taira (or Heike), fighting for supremacy at the end of the Heian period. In 1185, the Heike lost all at the battle of Dan-no-Ura Beach, where the child-emperor and his grandmother drowned, leaving the Dowager Empress Kenrei-mon-in as the only survivor of the Heike. She came to Jakko-in to become a nun because she failed to drown herself at Dan-no-Ura, having been rescued from the sea by a Genji soldier. She prayed the rest of her life at Jakko-in for the repose of the souls of her clan until she died at age thirty-six.[21] Since then, the Jakko-in has been a nunnery run by a long succession of ladies of high nobility. Therefore, Ohara remains a nostalgic memento of important episodes in early Japanese history long ingrained in the national memory. Curiously enough, Ohara has escaped massive tourist invasion, and is today still a tranquil and lovely village [PANELS 65–67]. Local farm women (*Ohara-me*), noted for their ancient regional dress, occupy their spare time with various handicrafts [PANEL 29L]. Delicious pickled vegetables grown in the valley have been renowned for centuries [PANEL 67]. There are few other villages in Japan as captivating as Ohara for the range of its Gentle Ways.

The other two most photographed country places in this book, Kanazawa-Bunko and Kamakura, also have an impressive historical background. Kanazawa-Bunko has the second oldest library in Japan founded in the thirteenth century by Sanetoki Hojo, the grandson of a regent of the Kamakura shogunate. It was rebuilt in 1930 on the spot where it had always been. It is situated by an oval pond in the enclosed garden of the small Shomyogi Temple [PANEL 28L], which has taken care of the library ever since 1333, when it lost contact with the Hojo family. Kanazawa-Bunko was a seaside village community in 1955; it is now filled with modern tract houses and is part of the huge Tokyo urban sprawl extending west to Yokohama and beyond. It is also located five miles from the large Naval base of Yokosuka, where I served as a Navy doctor in 1955–1956. During that time I stayed with my new Kyoto bride in an old Japanese inn, Kanazawa-en, on the shores of Oppama Bay, a little nook in the greater Tokyo Bay. For eighteen months, I had the good fortune to observe firsthand a traditional Japanese household (*ie*) and the surrounding village life rich in local Gentle Ways [PANELS 55,56,61,62,64].

The Kamakura region is one of the most important in Japanese history. Eight miles by road to the west of Kanazawa-Bunko, Kamakura is the country site where in 1192, a powerful military clan, the Minamoto, set up the first Japanese military government (or shogunate)

and became in effect a second capital. It ruled over fifteen eastern provinces at a time when the Fujiwara Emperors in Kyoto had become ineffective, and the glorious Heian era was drawing to a close.[21] Kamakura abounds in ancient crafts making armor, swords, lacquerware, and ceramics. After Nara, the Kamakura period was the Golden Age of Sculpture in Japan. The Bronze Buddha was cast in 1252 and is the second largest in the nation after the Great Buddha of Nara. Fine arts, literature, painting and the theater arts flourished in Kamakura. All of it was superb and stimulating, but very little belonged to the realm of the familiar except a long list of yearly festivals, and perhaps also "Kamakura Bori, a rustic style of wood carving in high relief then lacquered black and red."[20]

It was also to Kamakura that Zen Buddhism first came from China in the twelfth century. In the midst of often grandiose scenery, five magnificent Zen temples were built, of which only two remain today. Zen had been welcomed by the shogunate since the discipline and frugality advocated by Zen philosophy was well suited to the warrior class of the time. Except for a busy, small downtown area replete with art shops, Kamakura now is a large and varied natural park dotted with splendid temples, both Shinto [PANEL 45] and Buddhist. The extraordinary temple grounds and nearby areas always harbor a local life that is rich and vibrant, yet composed and gentle [PANELS 26,60L], as does the surrounding countryside [PANELS 10L,63].

PANEL 55 Above is the residence of one of the four sons of the Saita family owning the Kanazawa-en Inn. The new house was built on the grounds of the inn after the second son, Toku-jiro, became very successful in the aluminum business. He and his close school friend are trimming his inner court-yard trees on a Sunday afternoon; his aged mother, titular head of the household, came down from the inn to watch and visit with him. Her other three children each also built a house on the family grounds.

This photo shows preparations for a banquet given by
the household of Kanazawa-en in 1981 for our twenty-fifth
wedding anniversary and to celebrate our return visit to
the inn. My wife and I had lived there for eighteen months
in 1955–1956 while I served as a Navy doctor at the nearby
Yokosuka Naval Hospital.

PANEL 56   Above, Kamishibai (*kami*-paper, *shibai*-theater) is probably
no longer seen in Japan today. This was a precursor of
slide shows, using color images on paper to illustrate a
story. The storyteller would travel through the countryside
and stop in villages. He would set up a folding wooden
frame on the back of his bicycle and spin his tales, with
sound effects from his big drum, to a group of enthralled
small children. This is reminiscent of the *guignol*, a small
portable puppetshow set up at French countyfairs in premodern times. The photo was taken in 1955, near the entrance of Kanazawa-Bunko, where a sidestreet takes off
from the Yokohama-Yokosuka Road.

In Japan, land is as scarce as it is expensive. Many city or village dwellers buy a small plot not too far from their homes to grow their own vegetables. This is still true to-day in many parts of Europe and the Orient. These garden plots are getting scarcer in Kanazawa-Bunko which is gradually being swallowed by the Tokyo-Yokohama urban sprawl, inexorably moving down the coast of Tokyo Bay (1981).

PANEL 57   Korakuen Park is one of Japan's three most famous parks
and is located in Okayama [*see text*, PANELS 1–31]. In a
section of that park Japanese tea culture as practiced for
centuries can still be seen, unchanged (1985).

130

The old couple here in Japanese dress was photographed in front of a souvenir shop on the island of Miyajima in the Inland Sea (1956). This extremely beautiful island, one of the three most renowned scenic spots in Japan, is about thirty minutes by ferry from Hiroshima. Miyajima is easily noticeable from the sea because of its huge offshore vermillon *torii* which—as the shrine itself—seems to float on water at high tide. The island shrine is dedicated to the children of Susano-o-no-mikoto, the troublesome brother of the Sun Goddess, Amaterasu-o-mikami [*see text, Chapter III and* PANEL 28R].

131

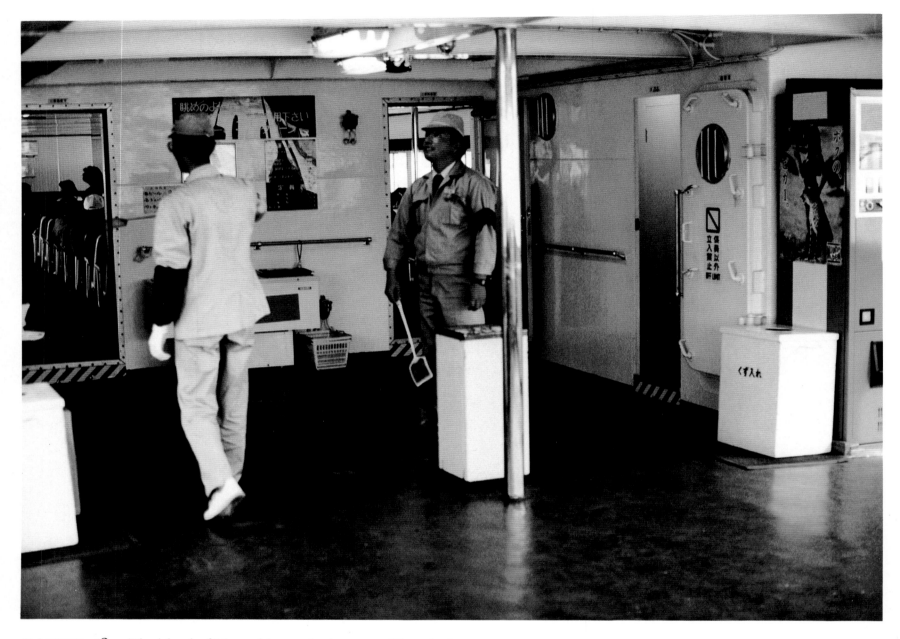

PANEL 58 The island of Matsushima—the last one of Japan's three most beautiful scenic spots—lies in an archipelago of many small pine-covered islands (*matsu*-pine, *shima*-island), and is about an hour's ride by ferry from Sendai, an important northern city. Matsushima has impressive cypress forests and a celebrated temple, Zuigan-ji, founded in the ninth century by the Tendai Buddhist sect but now the best known Zen temple in Northern Japan.[20] The fly-swatters above on the ferry's deck remind one of some surrealist ballet! Their caps have the same shape as those of World War II Japanese soldiers (1985).

Arashiyama is a favored excursion spot near Kyoto [*see next* PANEL]. Taken in 1956, the family photo above shows that modern women no longer follow the prewar custom of carrying both bundles and babies on family outings.[5]

PANEL 59   Arashiyama, a beautiful river spot thirty minutes drive
from Kyoto, has been a favorite excursion spot since Heian
emperors first enjoyed floating down the River Oi on long
wooden boats. The waters are crowded with visitors, not
only at cherry-blossom or maple-leaf viewing times, but
pretty much all year long. There are many residences and
restaurants bordering the river. Above is the lovely garden
at Kogo's (1987).

The long wooden boats of Arashiyama are reminiscent of the gondolas in Venice. The lady vendor shown on her boat is displaying some Japanese delicacies, candy and fruit to visitors in other boats going down the river (1987).

PANEL 60   Even today one sees wonderful people in the oddest little eating places throughout Japan. The old lady above, with classic features and grave bearing, was eating her *udon* (a standard Japanese lunch of noodles in broth with a variety of possible additives) in a very small noodle shop facing the train station in Kita-Kamakura (1987).

136

This fisherman with his jovial and calm expression is having a similar lunch of *udon* in Miyajima-guchi, a small port on the Inland Sea close to Hiroshima. The ferry ride to Miyajima takes about half an hour [*see text*, PANEL 57] (1985).

PANEL 61 Both photographs show offshore seaweed harvest. This is an ancient food gathering process of great importance to the Japanese because seaweed is used in many different ways as a condiment and was formerly useful as a source of iodine. Seaweed gathering consisted first in planting rows of posts into the sea bottom near the shore, then connecting these with nets at a measured height off the ground so that at hightide they would be below the water level. As the tide receded, seaweeds would be retained in those nets and then gathered with forks from flatbottom boats.

Later, the seaweeds were laid out to dry on rice-straw racks facing the sun and close to the water's edge [*fore-ground*] or in nearby fields. Seaweeds that had not settled in the nets as the tide receded could then be gleaned by hand from the shallow sea by needy women. They would either sell what they had gleaned or keep it for themselves. Before Japan's present affluence, scarcity and relative poverty were permanent conditions of life for many people, as was the case—and still is—in most of the Orient and Third World countries. (Both photos were taken in 1956.)

PANEL 62   At very low tide, the seaweed beds described in the previous PANEL can be seen clearly. Both photos are taken in 1955 on the beach front at Kanazawa-en Inn, on a warm summer day when seaweed gathering is at a low point. However, conditions are then perfect for clam digging. The U.S. Seventh Fleet big carrier seen in the distance [*above*] casts a striking note in an otherwise very peaceful scene.

Today, these seaweed beds have been displaced about a mile out into the bay waters facing Kanazawa-Bunko, as coastal land has been filled to make room for more industrial and residential space. A huge recreational beach park now stands on the area once covered by the sea and seaweed beds seen in both pictures. Similar land fills can be seen all around Tokyo Bay and elsewhere along the Japanese coastline. Ecological destruction of such magnitude would be hard to imagine in the United States at the present time.

PANEL 63 Hayama is a seaside resort close to Kamakura (*see text, Chapter IV*). It has splendid beaches [*both photos*], packed with swimmers in the long hot summers. Until recently, these beaches were deserted in the winter. Their vast expanses were used by local farmers and fishermen for a variety of purposes. Above, a fisherman and his two boys are all dressed up for the New Year's Day celebration in 1956.

Also photographed in 1956, huge white radishes are drying on a rack in the sun prior to being pickled and sold. On the ground there are also neat rows of salted fresh fish laid out to dry for several days, then to be sold for general consumption. Salted dry fish can be kept for a week or so without refrigeration. It is much in demand not only because of its ease of preparation—once heated it can be eaten as is—but because some varieties are prized as delicacies [PANEL 83].

PANEL 64 Next to Kanazawa-Bunko, on the other side of a short narrow tunnel, lies the fishing village of Koshiba. Above, an ancient crank is used by two fishermen to haul a boat onto the beach. On the right, red nets have been hung to dry in the wind.

The child eating "ice candy" and strapped to his mother's back [*right*] is about 30 months old. Thus, the child is close to his mother's body longer than in other cultures. Conversely, the mother is not separated from her children by the painful process of weaning.[11]

Both photos were taken in July 1962 right after sunset. An hour or so before, the fishing boats' varicolored tints were reminiscent of those of Van Gogh and Gauguin. Today, Koshiba has a modern harbor with a long concrete jetty and many new houses on filled land, a sign of the local population's recent prosperity.

PANEL 65 PANELS 65–68 depict Gentle Ways in the small fertile valley of Ohara, a unique village in the northwestern outskirts of Kyoto, well known since Heian times (ninth–thirteenth centuries) [*see text, Chapter IV*]. Curiously enough, Ohara has avoided massive tourist invasion and the garish buildings that go with it. It has remained a tranquil and bucolic farming village.

Ohara stretches beyond its valley on the lower slopes of Mount Hiei and ascends on the opposite side to the temple of Sanzen-in first established in the eighth century as a Tendai monastery. Its founder Saicho is famous in history for having brought this sect from China and for his role in the earliest Japanization of Buddhism [*see text, Chapter IV*]. Sanzen-in is now a Zen temple with extraordinary gardens. The surrounding area has some restaurants and shops selling local handicraft and other souvenirs.

PANEL 66 A winding narrow country road climbs from the bottom
of Ohara Valley to the temple of Sanzen-in [*see text*, PANEL
65]. A woman shopkeeper is washing the road facing her
front stall. She is using a long handled scoop in a way
probably identical to that used by her ancestors a thousand
years ago.

A housekeeper is returning home along the same road in mid-morning after her shopping. (Both pictures were taken in 1987.)

The usual ordinary meal in Japan consists of rice and tea with pickled vegetables. These condiments are also most appreciated by the Japanese at the end of any meal. In those places where pickled vegetables are particularly delicious, as in the countryside around Kyoto, customers may be invited to taste them at open storefronts. Left, an Ohara pickle vendor offers a passerby some of his specialties to taste at his front stall, much as American supermarket shoppers may be invited to taste a particular food sample on a given day.

Above, another well stocked pickle-and-tea specialty store in the farming village of Ohara, on the way to Sanzen-in. The smiling lady shopkeeper offers tea in front of her store to invite people to come in and look around. The Sanzen-in is a renowned temple of the old Tendai sect founded by the priest Saicho in the eighth century [PANELS 65, 69]. (Both photos were taken in 1987.)

PANEL 67

PANEL 68 The Jakko-in is a small ancient temple on a wooded slope in a most beautiful setting. It was first dedicated in A.D. 594 by Prince Shotoku who was the founding father of the Japanese state in the Asuka period, and it later became a Tendai temple. It was also the ultimate refuge of the last member of the Heike (or Genji) clan in their epic fight with the Minamoto clan at the battle of Dan-no-ura Beach in 1185. "In that fateful conflict where the Heike lost all, the Dowager Empress Kenrei-mon-in was the only Heike survivor". She came to Jakko-in to become a nun, and "prayed the rest of her life for the repose of the souls of her clan, until her death at age thirty-six".[21]

Since then, the Jakko-in has been a nunnery run by a long succession of ladies of high nobility, and Ohara has remained a nostalgic milestone of important events in early Japanese history.

The exquisite beauty of the small wooden gate in front of the temple above and the kimono clad visitor at right, almost gliding down the garden path, are in keeping with the bucolic and pastoral mood pervading all of Ohara.

152

PANEL 69 The cherry tree is a national symbol in Japan. Such trees may be seen in the gardens of most inns, temples and shrines. At cherry-blossom time, usually in April, their beauty is as exquisite as it is ephemeral, a theme much loved by the Japanese. The very large cherry tree above is in the garden of Kanazawa Inn, on the shores of Oppama Bay, a wide nook in the immense Tokyo Bay (1956). In the distance can be seen two rows of seaweed beds with a white fishing boat between them [*see* PANELS 62–63, *and text Chapter IV*]. In the background, to the left of the wooded hill falling abruptly into the sea, is the outline of a large Sumitomo factory.

On the right is a different kind of cherry tree, untended, with branches and blossoms cascading down to the ground (1987). It is on Mt. Hiei, in the enclosure of a cluster of temples close to the celebrated monastery of Enryaku-ji, "built near the site where Dengyo Daichi, or Saicho, first built a hut for meditation when he climbed Mt. Hiei in the year 788. The monastery's Primary Central Hall (Kon-ponchu-do) is a place of ritual practice for the protection of the nation. Before the main altar, three lamps known as the 'inextinguishable Dharma Lights', have been burning ceaselessly for the past twelve hundred years". Saicho, who introduced the Tendai sect from China in the eighth century was the first to liberalize ascetic Chinese Buddhism as practiced in Nara. He also established a school on Mt. Hiei which for centuries has exerted "tremendous influence not only on Buddhism but on Japanese culture and thought" (*from a leaflet at Mt. Hiei*).

A small statue of Jizo, the popular Buddha of children, is seen in the background with a bright red hat and bib. Remembrance of Jizo consists of placing stones in front of the statue to help the souls of children in the netherworld [*see text, Chapter IV*].

 CITY LIFE

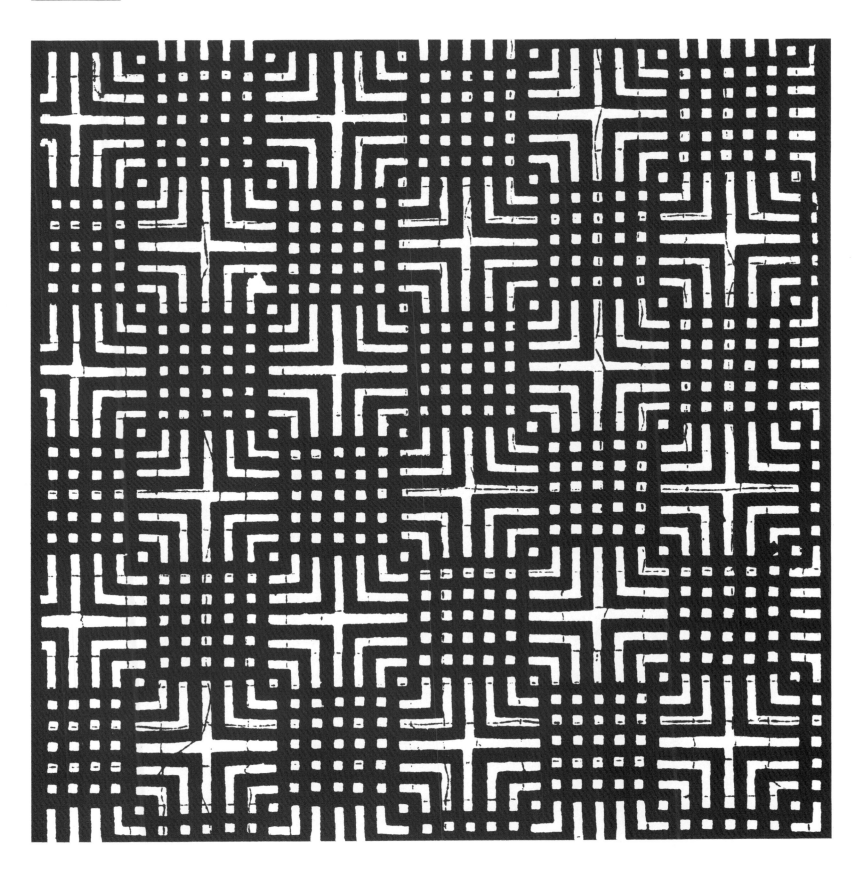

JAPANESE CITIES do not on the whole compare with Western cities except for the vast urban sprawls of Tokyo, Osaka and Kita-Kyushu, each an amorphous megalopolis devoted to heavy industry and modern technology. Moreover, many Japanese cities have been entirely rebuilt after the War and are often dismal complexes of ferroconcrete like Nagoya and Kawasaki in the center, Sendai and Sapporo in the north. Yet Hiroshima, levelled flat by the first Atomic Bomb, was beautifully restored [PANELS 93, 94], and Kyoto ("The Florence of the Orient") was alone untouched by war bombings. In spite of extensive rebuilding, most large cities have not lost the pattern of old traditional social structures, and except for their downtown areas, have remained agglomerations of small villages to an amazing extent. Tokyo which was destroyed twice in this century, first by an earthquake and then by war, has been largely rebuilt "on the old pattern of feudal times."[1] The Japanese have always preferred the closeness of the small group to be found "in neighborhood, kinship or teamwork" which continues to form the backbone of all Japanese life. Perhaps it is this closeness which is responsible for the small group's smoother efficiency. Nowhere is this more important than in the impersonal context of business life in large cities.

The Japanese, therefore, seem "reluctant to leave the sphere of common life. They are anxious to realize the maximum of social coherence and homogeneity, not of individual strength and glory. Thus, whatever they have produced, has entered the life of the ordinary man to an extent rarely seen in the West."[11] Whether in domestic products which flood world markets, or in decorative style which permeates most Japanese homes, the average man is made to feel he has a place, no matter how small, in the life of the nation. As a result, many aspects of the familiar are common to all, and may be recognized in the city as they are in the country, casting a glow of grace and cosiness on much of ordinary life.

Most of the photos on **City Life** have been taken in Kyoto, which remains the "spiritual capital of Japan."[5] In this last chapter, as elsewhere in the book, Gentle Ways in **City Life** have been grouped around four broad topics: **city shrines and streets**, **restaurants**, **shopping**, and **entertainment** including coffee houses,

bars, cherry blossom viewing, and the Miyako Odori, an annual spring dance in Gion, a famous Kyoto geisha district. The random distribution of many small Shinto shrines or sanctuaries throughout the streets of Kyoto and other Japanese cities is one of the more fascinating aspects of the country [PANELS 70,71,73R,74,38,39]. The Kitano Shrine in Northwestern Kyoto is an unusual, large sanctuary, popularly known as "Kitano Tenjin" and dedicated to the memory of Sugawara Michizane, an influential Heian court noble in the late ninth century [PANEL 35]. The rising Fujiwaras were "jealous of Michizane's position and succeeded in having him unjustly exiled to the island of Kyushu, where he died."[19] According to legend, "his death in 903 was followed by such severe earthquakes and storms in Kyoto, that in order to appease his spirit, a sanctuary was erected to enshrine him as a god to be named Tenjin."[20] In 947, the sanctuary was established with Imperial blessing. Seven centuries later, the last shogun before the Tokugawas, Toyotomi Hideyoshi, willed before his death that his son build a new shrine. This was done in 1607, and the imposing new buildings—still present today—are now registered as a National Treasure [PANEL 71L]. To commemorate these events, a fair continues to be held on the shrine grounds, the twenty-fifth of every month since ancient times [PANELS 71,81].

Many examples of the familiar can be seen on Buddhist temple grounds in Kyoto. These are favorite meeting places for children and adults alike [PANELS 4L,5R,18L]. An ancient Japanese custom calls for retainers or volunteer workers in the gardens of hallowed places as Mt. Hiei [*see introduction to* **Country Life**], or on the grounds of the Imperial Palace in the center of downtown Tokyo [PANEL 27]. A wonderful and soothing sight in some cities are old, small memorial shrines in a deserted street or on a wooded hill as in Kyoto [PANEL 74], or then a tranquil river bank as in Kurachiki [PANEL 75]. This is a seventeen century agglomeration renovated in the style of the period, somewhat like a Japanese Williamsburg but dedicated entirely to folk arts and surrounded by Okayama, a large industrial city.

The streets in Japan, as in many other Oriental or Latin societies, are often the center of daily life because in those countries urban dwellings are quite small and used mostly for sleeping and eating. Therefore, the streets of Japanese cities—and more so in Kyoto—can be an abundant source of Gentle Ways, perhaps best perceived when strolling along without any particular purpose. Downtown streets with their multicolored signs and shops are rarely garish, even in daytime [PANEL 72,9R]. Ordinary storefronts are often of subtle taste and aesthetic design [PANEL 76,93]. Shopping can be a fascinating experience, whether in Kyoto [PANELS 81−83,92R], Tokyo [PANEL 92L], Beppu [PANEL 91], or elsewhere. The Nishiki Food Market in Kyoto is exceptional, as are many other special food shops [PANEL 83]. These furnish regular fare as well as delicacies for special events [PANEL 84]. Schoolgirls of all ages everywhere to be seen are delightful for their gentleness, their spontaneity, their sweet innocence. This was as true thirty-five years ago [PANELS 4,5L,6,9] as it was in 1981 [PANELS 12R,22L,49R], in 1985 [PANELS 2,3,4R,12L], and today in 1987 [PANELS 9R,13R,34,73L]. The same generally applies to schoolboys [PANELS 56L, 4,5R,6L,7, 8L, 13L]. The theme of schoolgirls by groups of four or more in 1981 [PANEL 12R] is repeated in 1985 [PANELS 3, 12L] and in 1987 [PANELS 13R, 73L] to stress how very little apparent change has occurred in those six years. By contrast, schoolgirls of the same age in some Western countries look old before their time and often wear sloppy or "far out" clothes with heavy makeup and brightly painted nails, either to conform to an obscure notion of adult glamour or to emulate the psychopathology of the latest rock idol. Far more disturbing is that during the same period 1981−1987, too many of the public schools now attended by these Western girls and boys have been undermined by "widespread drug and alcohol abuse, pregnancy, suicide, robbery, assault, burglary, arson, and bombings" (*Time Magazine*, February 1, 1988).

City parks and streets can also be the site of entertainment—not only at important seasonal events such as maple-viewing in the fall and cherry-blossom viewing in the spring, both very ancient customs [PANEL 40]—but at many festivals throughout the year [PANEL 41] [*see introduction to Chapter III:* **Customs**]. Age-old ritual dances are routinely performed at major Shinto shrines at given times and for a small fee [PANEL 42], as well as during important holidays such as the New Year celebration [PANEL 45]. Theater and variety shows are available in every city, but of the more classic forms of entertainment only Osaka's famous puppet show (Bunraku) and Kyoto's traditional annual geisha dances are evocative of Gentle Ways.

As pointed out in Chapter II, the number of geishas, Japan's classic entertainers, is steadily decreasing because they have just become too expensive for most businessmen. Geishas are not prostitutes, but have been trained since childhood to become professional entertainers, as would ballet dancers. It takes at least ten years and often longer for a young girl to develop the required exquisite grace, manners and competence in conversation, song, dance and musical instruments to become a geisha. Starting at age six, she may become a *Maikosan*—a position similar to junior geisha—at about age thirteen. Given ability and luck, with the help of a rich enough patron to pay for evermore expensive brocade kimonos and other attire, she may become a full fledged geisha around age eighteen. During all this time and beyond, she lives in a geisha house with a few other young trainees under the supervision of an older geisha, much as an American girl might live in a sorority on or near the campus of her college. By the same token, the houses in a given geisha district give an annual dance (*odori*), usually in the spring, pretty much like girls in an American school might produce a yearly play or variety show. The three remaining geisha districts in Kyoto producing an annual show are: Gion, Pontocho, Kitano. Their annual spring dances are called Miyako, Kamogawa and Kitano Odori respectively. PANELS 85−87 show the Gion District's decorated main street in April 1956 with scenes of the Miyako Odori in 1956 and again in 1987.

The old Pontocho District [PANEL 88−90] also features many geisha houses (*okiya*), teahouses (*ochaya*) and bars. Customers will go into an *ochaya*, and ask for a particular geisha from a nearby *okiya* to come and entertain their party. There are also some bars in the narrow Pontocho Street. City bars (*see Chapter II*) are small, dimly lit, cozy places—much cheaper than *ochayas* with geishas—where men gather with a few friends after work to drink and talk and unwind: "Here the bar hostess, successor to the geisha tradition, engages them in amusing, titillating conversation,"[5] generally without any consequences. More such bars can be found in back streets of Japanese cities than in any other country.[10]

There are now innumerable coffee houses in the main streets of Japanese cities. It is a pleasant and relaxing experience to sit and watch the world go by in those small, aesthetically designed, very modern places, which also serve on occasion delicious small pastries in the richest continental tradition. In Chapter III, we have already seen the fundamental importance of food in Japanese life, and we touched upon the great variety of available restaurants. From a spotless sushi bar in Kyoto reminiscent of Shinto purity [PANEL 36L], to the exquisite food preparation in Yokohama's comfortable Kimpei [PANEL 46,48], and the elegant kneeling waitress saying good-bye outside the small, quaint stone garden at the entrance of Tokyo's expensive Egawa [PANEL 47R], we saw as many examples of Gentle Ways in Japanese restaurants.

Many popular eating places serving various kinds of noodles, broiled eel or tempura (deep-fried fish and vegetables) are inviting and have artistic appeal [PANEL 76]. Kyoto's large Ganko restaurant features not only fascinating food and fish displays [PANEL 78] but also a long sushi bar with keen master chefs who have been trained in the art of preparing raw fish for as long as ten years [PANEL 77]. The simple table settings of a place serving nothing but Japanese crepes [PANEL 79] can be as stunning in elegance as the more elaborate ones seen in Kyoto's best restaurants [PANEL 80]. More

modest establishments, where ladies alone often have a light dinner after shopping or in the early evening [PANEL 97] complete the list of eating places I have shown. In all of them, many facets of Japanese design and aesthetics create a decor from the ordinary to the luxurious, that remains very much in tune with the more comfortable and familiar aspects of life. In addition, PANELS 94–96 depict other gentle aspects of **City Life**.

Finally, there is the magnificent park built as a War Memorial to the atomic bomb victims in Hiroshima. This park is also a symbol of the most moving Gentle Way in Japan, a unique blend of the prehistoric Shinto quest for renewal and the ancient Buddhist concept of perpetual rebirth in a pervasive yet serene plea for eternal Peace [PANELS 98, 99].

PANEL 70 Some of the more fascinating aspects of Japan are small
Shinto shrines found at random in the streets of Kyoto
and other cities. Ladies in traditional Japanese dress were
frequently seen in town some thirty-five years ago. One
can still see them today, but to a lesser extent [PANELS 10L,
24L, 25, 68R]. The kimono clad ladies seen here are passing
in front of the Kumano Jinsha in Sakyoku, a residential
district of Kyoto.

The ladies shown above are in the courtyard of a small Shinto shrine off Shijo Street, a large thoroughfare in downtown Kyoto. The rows of hanging paper lanterns (*chochin*), usually lit at night, display ads for many shops and restaurants (1955).

This is eternal Japan! A Shinto shrine was founded in Kyoto more than a thousand years ago to the memory of a Heian court noble, Sugawara Michizane, who was unjustly exiled and later deified as "Tenjin"! This sanctuary, the Kitano Shrine, was rebuilt under a famous shogun in the seventeenth century, and the splendid main structure was since registered as a National Treasure. In its inner sanctum there are incredibly beautiful thirteenth and fourteenth century scrolls recounting an illustrated history of the shrine.

To commemorate these events, a fair has been held on the shrine grounds the twenty-fifth of every month since ancient times, and it still is. There is always a large, motley crowd at the fair, and sooner or later everyone stops in front of the shrine to worship. This is most simple: Clap your hands or ring the bell by pulling the rope in front of the shrine to wake up the somnolent god (*kami*), bow humbly a minute or two, then put a coin into the wooden

hopper in lieu of the symbolic offering of food or drink, and follow with a short prayer. Shinto priests normally go through a purification ritual before morning worship. Above, early in the morning before crowds arrive at the fair, Kitano Shrine priests are walking toward the main sanctuary building after the head priest purified them by waving a wand of white paper streamers seen clearly in background on a table next to the stone lion. These streamers are symbolic of ancient offerings of rice and cloth.

PANEL 71

PANEL 72

166

The streets in Japan, as in many other Oriental or Latin societies, are often the center of daily life because in these countries urban dwellings are generally quite small and used for little more than sleeping and eating.

Above, the corner of Nijo and Kiyamachi dori, a lovely street bordering a quiet stream, shows a close-up of a small apartment house and several other colorful shops.

Right, a small stretch of Kiyamachi Street near the Kamo River in Kyoto shows an amazing array of densely packed shops and restaurants. From front to back we see a tea-room (Savoy), a French restaurant (Ogawa), a Japanese inn (Kisen), a Chinese restaurant serving *gioza* or potstickers (*hanten*), an *udon* or noodle shop, another restaurant (Ikura) and a pet shop (Inuneko).

167

PANEL 73 Five junior high school girls in Nara visit the Horyu-ji Temple, the most ancient wooden structure in Japan dating back to the Asuka period in the sixth century. The theme of these sweet, gentle and innocent school girls first seen in 1955 [PANELS 6, 9], then in 1981 [PANEL 12R], and again in 1985 [PANEL 12L] is repeated here once more in 1987 because it is such an important feature of Japanese life, manifest everywhere throughout the country. These young girls are still looking forward to having a husband and raising a family when they grow up, and this bodes well for the future mental health of the nation.

The small Shinto shrine (shown here in 1987) surrounded by shops in the heart of Kyoto displays innumerable ads on its many paper lanterns, much as the one seen in PANEL 70 thirty-two years earlier. The location of these multiple small shrines in the midst of crowded downtown areas is reminiscent of Chinese Taoist temples which serve as community centers, where people not only offer brief prayers, but meet and chat. There are often small shops and food counters on the very temple grounds, with quite a din on market days when the aroma and fumes of the incense burners mix with those of the kitchen! Taoist temples are now seen mostly in Taiwan and other areas throughout the Orient with large Chinese populations. [Taoism is a pragmatic Chinese religion akin to *laissez-faire*, most prevalent in South China and derived from the writings of Lao-Tse (b. 603 B.C.). It offered welcome relief from the rigors of Northern Confucianism. Taoism later blended with Indian meditative Buddhism to become Zen].

169

PANEL 74   A soothing and often nostalgic sight in some cities, and notably in Kyoto, are small memorial shrines tucked away on quiet streets or hidden in wooded hills. Near the temple of Kyomizu in Kyoto, stands an especially beautiful and simple sanctuary (Hokoku-byo) dedicated to the memory of Toyotomi Hideyoshi, the last great ruler of Japan before the advent of the Tokugawas who controlled Japan with an iron hand for nearly three centuries (1955).

170

In a deserted Kyoto sidestreet is this small unidentified shrine (photographed in 1955), not far from the Sanju-sangendo. The soft design of the roof and stairs in the admirable natural setting convey the tranquil mood of eternal repose.

PANEL 75   Kurashiki is a seventeenth century city close to Okayama
on the Sanyo line, which runs from Kobe to the island of
Kyushu on the north shore of the Inland Sea. Kurashiki is
connected to the sea by a river, and in the Edo period it
was a thriving port for the shipment of rice produced in
this district. Rice was stored in several government run
local granaries, hence the name Kurashiki which means
"the seat of granaries".[20] It is now an important textile city,
but is noted primarily for its very active cultural center almost entirely due to the philanthropist Ohara who established several fine museums near the canal. Three museums
(one of which is shown above) are located in old rice granaries, elegantly restored in the architecture of the period.[21]

172

In this sense, Kurashiki's cultural center could be called a small Japanese Williamsburg. There is a famous Folk Art Museum which is best known for the rich variety of popular handicrafts in many parts of Japan. There is also a small but excellent archaeological museum with various ceramics and other treasures of prehistoric Japan (Yayoi, Jomon, Kofun periods) and of China going back to the Tang Period. In addition to a well known museum of Impressionist art, there is a remarkable small museum of modern Japanese ceramics. A striking permanent exhibit of modern Japanese painters (Umehara, Hayashi, Fujita, etc.) is housed in a long, low modern building which fits in rather well with the ancient style of the other structures. The photo shows a tranquil river bank with a small restaurant and some stores reflected in the water. (Both photos taken in 1985.)

PANEL 76 There are many popular eating places serving various kinds of noodles, broiled eel, or tempura. These little restaurants are inexpensive but usually inviting and not devoid of aesthetic appeal. The one above (Kyoto, 1954), with a World War II vintage bicycle in front of it, shows small entrance door curtains (*noren*) floating in the wind and is probably just a counter place with a few tables [*see text, Chapter V*].

The tempura restaurant shown here displays plastic replicas of a great variety of combination plates in its front window (1955). Tempura is a fish and vegetable dish with a very light batter quickly deep-fried. It was imported to Japan by Portuguese traders in Nagasaki early in the sixteenth century.

PANEL 77 Ganko restaurant on Sanjo Street occupies an entire building complex. It is noteworthy that the early morning sidewalk washing process is essentially the same as that seen in the mountain village of Ohara [PLATE 66] except for using a hose instead of a scoop due to the larger area involved. It is of further interest that such a simple and rural activity is taking place on one of the principal streets of downtown Kyoto, a city of well over a million people. Similar old customs are in evidence in urban settings all over Japan.

Ganko has a very long sushi bar with small booths down-stairs and private dining rooms and banquet facilities on the upper floors. The sushi chef [*sushi-cho-kunin*] seen behind the bar is a master who has been trained for at least ten years in the art of preparing raw fish. An incredible variety of dishes are skillfully laid out and beautifully arranged in front of the customer, and are as delicious as they are decorative.

PANEL 78 Kyoto's large Ganko restaurant features fascinating fish and food displays, both in its front windows and behind its long sushi bar. (Both pictures were taken in 1987.)

178

179

PANEL 79 Nishimura is a small Kyoto restaurant which is situated in
a quaint garden and serves a large selection of Japanese
crepes (*okonomyaki*) in several private dining rooms.

180

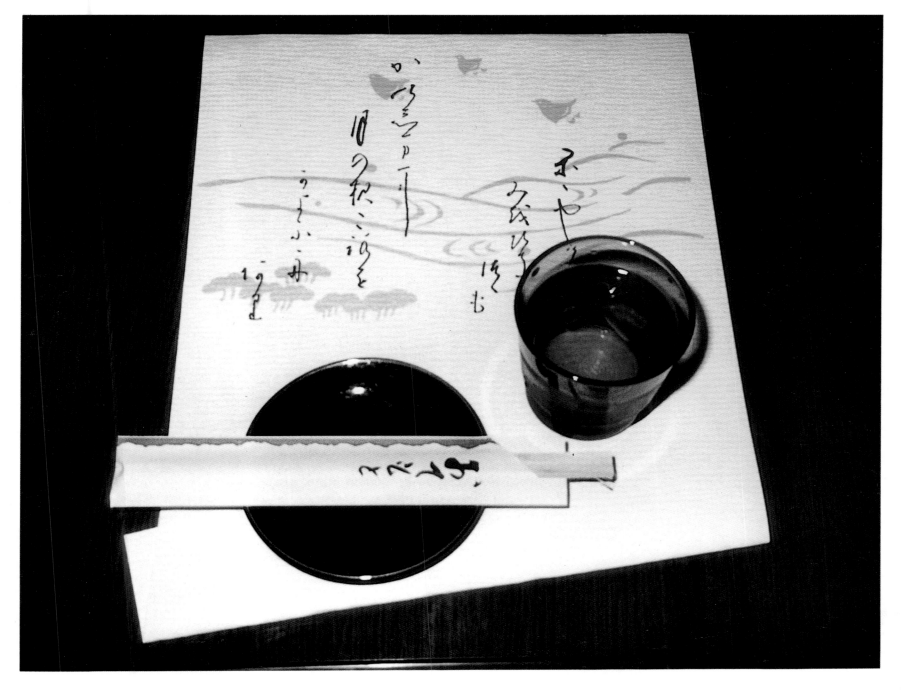

Nishimura's simple place setting, with a poem in both *hirangana* and *kanji* characters, is as stunning in its elegance as those of Higashiyama Villa, an expensive Kyoto establishment [*see next* PANEL].

PANEL 80 Both pictures show elegant, expensive Kyoto restaurants where the menu—always a la carte—does not give any prices, and dining is usually in private rooms.

Higashiyama [*above*] is an old villa on a wooded hill overlooking the city near the temple of Kiyomizu. A unique feature of dining at Higashiyama is that after the main courses, guests are taken to a second dining room where dessert and tea are waiting, beautifully set out on another low table. After dinner, the party may be taken for a visit of the owners' "storage house" filled with many art treasures (1981).

The smiling, well-dressed lady owner of Aya restaurant is shown with her chef. Aya is a small exclusive place in Sakyoku with a counter in the front and two private dining rooms in back. It serves delicate northern fish specialties from Hokkaido. As in all similar Japanese restaurants, guests in private dining rooms always sit on cushions at low tables aesthetically set up on tatami floors.

PANEL 81   The monthly fair held at the Kitano Shrine in Kyoto has very ancient origins [*see text,* PANEL 71]. On the twenty-fifth of every month the grounds of this unique Shinto sanctuary (which has several large stone *torii*) are overrun by innumerable vendors displaying their wares in closely packed stalls or sometimes on the pavement itself. The scene shown above is again typical of eternal Japan!

Right, much as in a flea market, a great variety of antiques, ceramics, used goods and often extraordinary objects are available.

184

PANEL 82   Ever since city fairs have existed, country folks from the
surrounding areas have brought their goods to town for
sale. Some fairs sell flowers, but all of them offer a variety
of foods, usually local specialties and delicacies.

It is a fascinating and sometimes even a poetic experience to stroll through the fairgrounds at the Kitano Shrine, as shown here by the pensive flower vendor and the wonderful country woman dispensing some pickled vegetables from her stall.

PANEL 83   The Nishiki Market is a long and narrow arcade which
runs through a large city block and joins two principal
streets in the center of Kyoto. On either side of this arcade
are a great many stalls with every kind of food available in
Japan arranged in the most colorful and artistic way.
Above, a large selection of dried fish is displayed in such
neat rows that they could pass military inspection (1981)!

Here is a more refined shop featuring the choicest pickled vegetables available in the city of Kyoto (1981). Again the layout and presentation have an aesthetic touch, as do the design and style of the store. The seemingly trivial theme of pickled vegetables is repeated here in an elegant downtown setting, not only because they form so varied and colorful an exhibit, but because they harken back two millenia to the very source of agriculture in Japan. Moreover, these condiments, first contrived by the ancient Japanese to preserve vegetables in all climates, are an essential part of everyone's daily fare, and indeed a primal part of the familiar in this nation. Every Japanese eats some pickles (*tsukemono*) with his bowl of rice for breakfast, just as a Westerner puts sugar in his coffee or butter on his bread.

189

PANEL 84 A peculiar feature of modern Japanese homes is that one of the front rooms must be fitted with Western furniture, usually of the ugliest and heaviest kind, reminiscent of the Victorian parlor. It is here that visiting friends and guests are received for tea and sweets.

This photograph shows the younger son of the Hirata household serving tea to three of his friends before an outing on a Sunday afternoon (1981). Rarely would such gentle formality be seen in a comparable age group in the West.

An average suburban family is starting a feast of sushi
and sukiyaki on a special occasion in their kitchen-dining
room, the usual eating place in most Japanese homes
(1985).

PANEL 85   Geisha are Japan's classic entertainers, but they are steadily decreasing in number because they have become too expensive for most businessmen. Geisha are not prostitutes but have been trained since childhood to become professional entertainers, as would ballet dancers. A young girl has to devote at least ten years to develop the required exquisite grace, manners, competence in conversation, song, dance and musical instruments to become a geisha. During this time and beyond she lives in a geisha house with other trainees under the supervision of an older geisha, much as an American college girl might live in a sorority house on or near campus [*see text, Chapter V*].

192

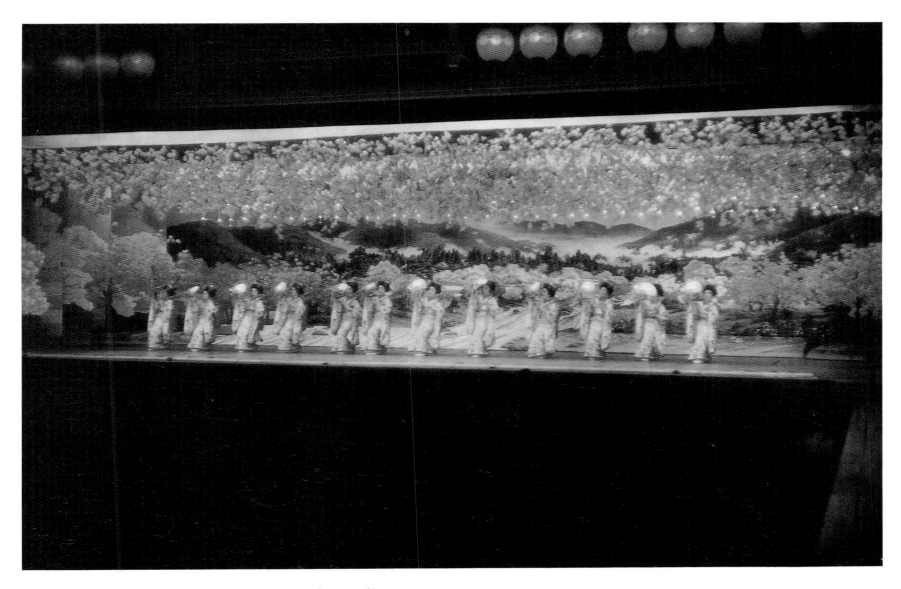

Several geisha houses may form a district, and some districts are naturally larger and more celebrated than others. Left, main street of the Gion geisha district in Kyoto decorated for its annual spring dance, the Miyako Odori, always held in the district's own theater for six weeks starting in early April (1956). The woman shown in the picture's lower right corner wears a mask so as not to spread her cold to others. This is a ubiquitous custom throughout Japan and other densely populated areas of the Far East, which the West could well emulate.

The stage of the annual Gion Miyako Odori in Kyoto (1956).

PANEL 86 Both photographs show scenes of the same Gion Miyako Odori (Cherry Dance) in the spring of 1987. "The dance is very beautiful, consisting of a series of graceful posturings to the music of an orchestra of samisen, flutes, drums and sometimes bells. The dancers are dressed in kimono of uniform style. The stage scenery, artistically designed, changes for each scene".[20]

Above, dancers enter the stage from a side gangway. On the right, is the orchestra of women playing the ancient three string Japanese guitar, the samisen.

194

PANEL 87   Before the Miyako Odori dance given each spring by the Gion geishas in their own district's theater [*see* PANELS 85, 86], theatergoers holding tickets for the better seats may assist at a large tea ceremony given by fully attired geishas and their younger assistants (*maiko* or *maikosan*)[20], such as the one above, in April 1956.

This photograph shows an identical tea ceremony at the Pontocho Theater in May 1988, when the geisha in that district give their annual spring dance, the Kamogawa Odori. While in both pictures the implements and gestures are the same as in the classical tea ceremony, what is seen here is more of an exhibit for a large group of people. Therefore, it is quite different from the original sixteenth century tea drinking ceremony with understated Zen overtones designed for meditation with a small number of persons in the intimate atmosphere of a rustic teahouse.

PANEL 88 The old Pontocho Street shown here in 1961 is Kyoto's second most important geisha district. At that time it still had many geisha houses and tearooms but also an increasing number of restaurants and small bars. The Pontocho District is on either side of the narrow street seen above and lies on the bank of the Kamo River between the Sanjo and the Shijo Bridges. The origin of the name "Ponto-cho" (Bridge District) may come from the Portuguese who had first visited Japan in the sixteenth century. The district also acquired fame in the nineteenth century through the celebrated drawings and woodblock prints of Hiroshige.

As discussed in the text and in PANEL 85, geisha—long Japan's classic entertainers—are decreasing in numbers because of the prohibitive cost of their services. To a large extent geisha houses and teahouses where geisha used to entertain parties of customers have been replaced by small city bars. These are "small, dimly lit, cozy places", much cheaper than tea houses with geishas, where men gather with a few friends after work to drink and talk and unwind. "Here the bar hostess, successor to the geisha tradition, engages them in amusing, titillating conversations. . . . The milieu may be different, but the spirit of these bars is close to that of the amusement center of Feudal times".[5] More such bars can be found in the backstreets of Japanese cities than in any other country.[10] Recently, however, these bars have mushroomed in the cities larger streets, such as Nawate-dori (seen at right in Kyoto, April 1988) where entire buildings are occupied by such bars.

198

199

Both photographs show the Pontocho geisha district at night in April 1988. On the left is a *maikosan* or junior geisha walking along the narrow street in classic attire and neck makeup (*eriashi*). Since ancient times, a beautiful neck on a woman has been an object of admiration, and the unique neck makeup shown here was designed for greater cosmetic effect and is worn only by *maikosan*. The woman seen in the shadow at the right of the picture and passing the junior geisha shows a certain amount of diffident appreciation and may or may not be working as a bar hostess.

The photo above shows a group of five Pontocho junior geisha at a meeting point before entering a restaurant or a teahouse to entertain what is certainly a group of well heeled customers. As such, the above picture is quite rare, since in this modern era, a group of fully dressed *maikosans* about to go to work can almost never be photographed together at night in the main street of a geisha district. The exhorbitant cost of the rich brocade and silk kimono worn by these *maikosan* is one of the reasons for their diminishing numbers and explains also why each of them needs a patron to subsidize, at least in part, their very expensive wardrobes.

This picture shows Kiyamashi-dori, a long and lovely Kyoto street which borders the Takasegawa Canal, and which for part of its course between the Sanjo and Shijo Bridges is parallel to Pontocho. The canal (not seen) is on the right of the picture, Pontocho Street is one block to the left and the tall structure in the middle with innumerable luminous signs is filled with as many small bars. It is noteworthy that a few minutes walk from where this photo was taken is a high and narrow building, one of many ultra-modern "love hotels" throughout Japanese cities which offer rooms for one or several hours, day or night. In view of the overcrowding, scarcity and very high cost of any housing in Japanese cities, a couple without any privacy of their own can hardly afford a two hundred dollar downtown hotel room for a short tryst or casual sex. Thus, "love hotels" fill a realistic need for any couple desiring a few hours' intimacy at affordable cost (1988).

Above is the owner-manager (*mamasan*) of a small Pontocho bar. There is a counter where five or six people could sit and as many small tables. Perhaps two to four bar hostesses may be working at any one time. Drinks are very expensive, and usually go by the half bottle of scotch. There is *karaoke* (or singing with taped stereophonic orchestral music) if customers so desire. The atmosphere is relaxed and pleasant. Any couple, married or not, who can afford the stiff tab of sixty to eighty dollars for a few drinks, is now welcome in such bars. As little as ten years ago, these bars were for men only. Hostesses are neither prostitutes nor call girls, but may in time befriend a customer. A hostess may have an affair with a customer and she may even get married. But her main function is to listen and to entertain; that is to be pleasant and amusing with one or several men so as to make them stay and drink long enough to satisfy the *mamasan*. Since most patrons are on an expense account, the *mamasan* is generally happy, as seen here (1988)!

PANEL 91 Both photos show the streets of Beppu on a midsummer night in 1955, when our ship, a troop transport (AKA 99 USS Rolette), stopped over for a day in the westernmost Japanese island of Kyushu. "Beppu is known throughout Japan for its hot springs which include alkaline, sulfur, iron and carbonated baths, all prescribed for various ailments. There are also hot sand baths on the beach where people half bury themselves in the sand".[20] There are eight spas and many boiling ponds of various bright colors according to the predominant chemicals; some are green, others are brick-red or blue. They are so hot that eggs easily boil in them. Some spout water and mud a foot high in the air. These are aptly called *jigoku,* meaning boiling ponds but also hell holes! Beppu has a great many inns and hotels, some of which are located on a large hill overlooking the city with a great view of the Bay. In 1955, the Suginoi Hotel high up on the hill was very attractive. The general atmosphere of these hot-spring hotels brings to mind the noted spas of Western Europe.

By contrast, the heart of the city has a more tropical flavor than the rest of Japan. The downtown area is filled with bazaars, shops, a maze of small streets and alleyways and the usual plethora of small bars, from the sleazy to the wonderful. Left, two girls, possibly twins, taking an evening stroll are dressed in *yukata* a light cotton kimono worn outside only in the heat of summer.

Above, a store window displays brightly colored bolts of cloth, while the owner sitting on his elevated tatami floor chats with a child-carrying woman standing in the entryway. The photo gives a good idea of the small entrance so characteristic of many Japanese homes and stores. It is usually at street level and allows for a visitor to talk with people in the house without actually coming in. It is only upon entering the room itself that shoes are removed and left on the entrance floor where the woman is seen standing. Except for downtown shops, offices, hotels, theaters and public buildings in large cities, removal of shoes on entering any house or dwelling is still the general rule in Japan today. Note a World War II vintage bicycle in front of the store (1955).

PANEL 92   Walking along the streets of Japanese cities without any
purpose other than to sightsee or window shop can be a
wonderful experience. Here, three rather severe Japanese
matrons in traditional dress settle their accounts after
lunch in the basement gallery of a recently finished large
Tokyo hotel (1987).

A bemused shop girl carefully dusts various teapots and other dainty pieces of pottery in a downtown Kyoto ceramics store (1987).

PANEL 93 Japanese storefronts are often of subtle taste and aesthetic design with clear, unpainted wooden lattice, deriving from the Sukiya style of architecture developed by Sen-no-Rykyu, the greatest Teamaster of all time. This architecture, as the tea ceremony itself, suggests the Zen preference for understated elegance, which is in effect "a simple expression of the essential".[18]

Shown here is a modern sushi-place front window in the center of Kyoto, exhibiting not only beautiful plastic replicas of the day's available selections but also many kinds of sushi tastefully arranged in a variety of attractive gift boxes. The half hidden *kanji* characters calligraphed on the sliding doors (*shoji*) in the background have a distinct Zen overtone.

208

This is a specialty store for tea ceremony implements. It exhibits a similar aesthetic Sukiya design, and displays a variety of refined objects used in the tea arts.

PANEL 94 Both photos show the race track at Kamigamo Shrine in Kyoto (May 1988) during the preparatory runs held the first Sunday of each month for the yearly race conducted on May 5, when "20 racers, dressed in full Heian court regalia, after worshipping at the shrine, participate in the historic horserace started in 1093 as a form of prayer for a good harvest".[20] The preparatory races have a peculiar format. The race tract is rectilinear and about 800 yards long. It is fenced off on both sides. There are public stands in the form of a simple, long, covered platform some two feet off the ground. On the other side of the field, the judges, who are also in Heian costume, sit on a higher platform with a more formal and elaborate roof. Several riders, each with his own attendant and other retinue on foot, parade their horses up and down the track before their turn to race comes up. They pass several times in front of the judges and the public stand. All riders wear Heian court costume while their horses are fitted with Heian period harness and stirrups. Some of these racers are quite young.

Each rider then charges down the track at full gallop yelling "sa!" at the top of his voice [*above*], and returns to the starting line by a road parallel to the track but outside the temple grounds. Individual riders make several runs during the afternoon. The judges then decide the relative standing of each rider at the end of each racing day, all in preparation for the yearly May 5 race when twenty men—in more splendid Heian regalia—charge down the full track together.

The Kamigamo Shrine is a most ancient Shinto sanctuary and is just as famous as the nearby Shimogamo Shrine. Both of these are the seat of the prominent Aoi Matsuri (Hollyhock Festival) held each year since the seventh century on May 15 to conciliate the gods of Thunder and Earthquakes![20] During this festival "hollyhock leaves, which were believed to prevent both thunder and earthquakes, are seen hanging under the eaves of homes and on the hats and floats of the festival participants".[26]

PANEL 95 Shinjuku Station in northern Tokyo's new skyscraper district is one of several mammoth railway stations in Japan and has the second largest passenger traffic in the Capital. The platform sign above is of interest because it indicates the name SHINJUKU in three alphabets: First there is the easily recognizable roman lettering for Westerners; immediately above and below are Chinese or *kanji* characters, and on top, in the biggest lettering, is the station's name in Hiragana. These characters are also used at the bottom of the sign for Nakana and Yotsuya under the directional arrows.

The Hiragana syllabary is historically important because it was developed as a simplified script from Chinese ideographs by Japanese court ladies and other poets between the eighth and the twelfth centuries, starting less than two hundred years after writing was first introduced from China. While composing such Japanese poems or *waka*, the imported *kanji* characters came to be used as phonetic symbols, which gave rise to two essentially Japanese Kana syllabaries of 52 characters each: Katakana and Hiragana. The former made daily script much easier; the latter facilitated poetic expression. Everyday written Japanese has since used a mixture of all three characters: Chinese or *kanji*, Hiragana, and Katakana. The latter alone does not figure on the above Shinjuku platform sign, but it does appear on many signs of places with longer or more complicated names.

212

This picture shows a Japan Railway train about to depart from Shinjuku Station in mid-morning after the rush hour period. These are the only suburban trains in the world in which there are no odors whatever, except some pleasant scent coming from the ceiling fans in warm weather. The spotless white gloves of the train conductor should be noted as well as the gleaming aspect of the car itself. There are no graffiti on trains and subways in Japan. These are the same trains which were celebrated in the international press several years ago when at rush hours conductors were photographed forcibly pushing the last passengers in cars to allow the train doors to close. It is remarkable that no matter how trying the circumstances, passengers remain polite and calm. It is even more remarkable that in 1988 when Shinjuku Station conveys three million passengers a day, there are no acts of violence, be it mugging, theft, assault or crime of any kind. In fact, the most that is usually recorded are a few cases of public drunkenness!

Both photographs show lovely hostesses at the recently opened (April 1988) "Grand Exhibition of Silk Road Civilizations" in Nara, the first capital city of Japan before the birth of Kyoto. These pretty young girls in blue and green uniforms (the colors of the Exposition) are seen at closing time near the main gate of the Kasugano exhibit area; first lining up, then, bowing deeply, while saying together in their sing-song voices "*Arrigato Gozaimashita*", the very polite form of "Thank you very much". The custom of employees bowing together to greet customers or to thank them on their departure is borrowed from large department stores in which as little as 20 years ago the entire staff would line up at the front door at opening time and greet the first shoppers with the most polite: "*Irrashai mase*" or "Be most welcome".

Even today in most large department stores beginning salesgirls are used as greeters near the front doors or at the bottom of escalators to bow deeply while saying sweetly "*Irrashai mase*" when customers arrive, and "*Arrigato Gozaimashita*" when they leave.

"The Silk Road" refers to several ancient commercial routes (Oasis, Steppe and Sea) connecting the eastern and western part of Asia over a distance of nearly 6000 miles. The Oasis Route, stretching from the Mediterranean to Xian in China, was the most celebrated of these roads during the Han to Tang periods for about a thousand years (second century B.C.—eighth century A.D.), a millenium corresponding to the Age of Rome, Byzantium and Sasanian Persia. The Silk Road was dotted with oases where travellers from various lands, having weathered untold dangers, gathered to form markets and trade goods. In time, caravan cities developed in these oases and provided welcome living conveniences plus facilities for long distance travel. Civilizations along the Silk Road included Western Mediterranean nations, the Ottoman Empire, the Soviet Union, Afghanistan, Pakistan, India, Mongolia with Central Asia, China, and later on Korea and Japan. Goods traded back and forth were mostly precious stones, many kinds of silk and brocade, gold and silverware, lacquer, bronze mirrors, clothes, musical instruments, paintings, sculptures, spices, medicines and countless handicrafts. It was on the Silk Road—celebrated centuries later by Marco Polo—that Buddhism spread from India to China [*from an Exhibition Catalog*].

PANEL 97 Because of their harrowing work schedule including several hours of commuting a day, many Japanese men don't come home until late in the evening. Thus, many wives with grown children, or single women, go out in pairs or alone for a light dinner. In spite of the ill-effects of intense urbanization to which 70% of Japanese are subjected with "extreme overcrowding due to permanent lack of space", city streets at night are still perfectly safe and routine muggings simply do not occur.

Relatively few foreigners are aware that in spite of new cars, televisions, and other postwar home improvements, the "Japanese standard of well-being is still relatively low, and people are really a lot poorer than statistics would indicate".[5]

Yet, the Japanese have fared better in the dehumanizing climate of the technological society than other modern nations. In fact, they have considerably less crime, less juvenile delinquency, less divorces, less drugs, less moral and social disintegration than any other major advanced industrial state. The reader who may be interested in possible causes for this remarkable success is referred to the Documentary Appendix.

Above, two girls in deep conversation at Kyoto's Ganko. Right, a lady is ordering her dinner at Takajiyo, an attractive but simple upstairs place serving various kinds of noodles and other standard Japanese fare. Takajiyo is opposite Sanjo Station near the Kamo River in Kyoto. (Both photos taken in 1987.)

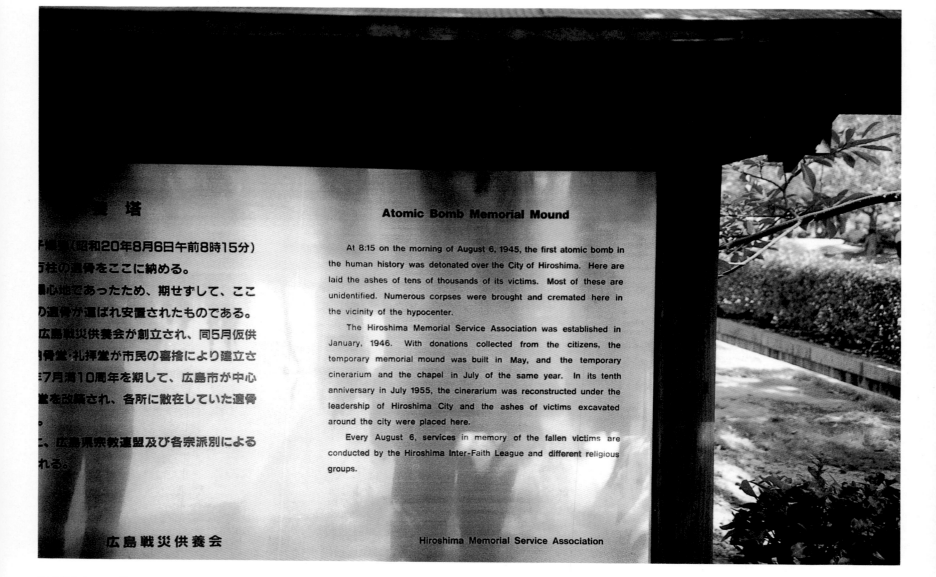

Atomic Bomb Memorial Mound

At 8:15 on the morning of August 6, 1945, the first atomic bomb in the human history was detonated over the City of Hiroshima. Here are laid the ashes of tens of thousands of its victims. Most of these are unidentified. Numerous corpses were brought and cremated here in the vicinity of the hypocenter.

The Hiroshima Memorial Service Association was established in January, 1946. With donations collected from the citizens, the temporary memorial mound was built in May, and the temporary cinerarium and the chapel in July of the same year. In its tenth anniversary in July 1955, the cinerarium was reconstructed under the leadership of Hiroshima City and the ashes of victims excavated around the city were placed here.

Every August 6, services in memory of the fallen victims are conducted by the Hiroshima Inter-Faith League and different religious groups.

Hiroshima Memorial Service Association

塔

午慰霊（昭和20年8月6日午前8時15分）
万柱の遺骨をここに納める。

心地であったため、期せずして、ここ
の遺骨が運ばれ安置されたものである。

広島戦災供養会が創立され、同5月仮供
骨堂・礼拝堂が市民の募捨により建立さ
7月満10周年を期して、広島市が中心
堂を改築され、各所に散在していた遺骨

に、広島県宗教連盟及び各宗派別による
れる。

広島戦災供養会

PANEL 98 The first time I saw Hiroshima was in August 1955 from the deck of a Navy ship steaming slowly towards the city which had been wiped out ten years before by the first Atomic Bomb. The ship's executive officer warned all those going ashore that this was one city where Americans were not welcome. He urged everyone "not to get into trouble". No one did. At that time, Hiroshima was still being rebuilt. Everywhere huge posters in both Japanese and English proclaimed the word "Peace". Near the ruin of the old prewar Industrial Hall [PANEL 99R] corresponding to the Bomb's "ground zero", there sat a man on a low stool next to a sign with the inscription: "Kiyoshi Kikkawa—Atomic Bomb Victim #1". For a very small fee, he would pull up his shirt and show his back, horribly scarred by deep thermal burns.

Thirty years later, a beautifully landscaped park had grown around the War Memorial and Atomic Bomb Museum, both already built in 1955.

218

This park is laid out on a long and narrow island in the middle of the river which runs through the length of the city, now wholly rebuilt, and particularly resplendent on a sunny day. At one pole of the oblong island stands the ruin of the Industrial Hall (A-Bomb Ground Zero). At the opposite pole, perhaps six hundred yards away, is the Atomic Bomb Museum [*see text*, PANEL 9], a sober modern structure, in front of which—dead center—rises the tunnelled roof of the cenotaph itself, patterned on a Haniwa prehistoric Japanese dwelling. Standing in front of this cenotaph (dedicated to the nearly two hundred thousand victims of the bomb) and looking through the tunnelled roof, one sees in the distance the ruin on "ground zero"—an overwhelming sight!

The memorial mound above is a tumulus, erected in the Park to tens of thousands of unidentified victims, and built in the tradition of the Kofun period (A.D. 300–552) when royalty and notables were buried in tumulus-shaped tombs copied from China and later Korea. The many clusters of multicolored paper streamers hanging from staffs and seen on the right of the photo, are made by school children or other groups, and like the flower offerings, are constantly renewed.

219

東京方... ...
ひろい世界を同じ心で一つに結ぶ、全世界のライオンズ
会員が平和実現のために果す役割りは大きい。
　原爆ドームの永久保存に呼応し、人類が初の原爆の洗礼
を受けた時刻、8時15分に、毎日全世界に向けこの時計
塔のチャイムが「ノーモアヒロシマ」を強く訴え、人類の
恒久平和実現の一日も早からんことを祈り、この時計塔を
建設し、市に贈るものである。

昭和42年10月28日
チャーター伝達10周年を記念し
広島鯉城ライオンズクラブ

平和の時計

PEACE CLOCK TO

QUARTER PAST EIGHT EVERY MORNING, THE MORTAL MOMENT OF THE BLASTING
BACK IN 1945, THE CLOCK WILL CHIME ITS PRAYER FOR PERPETUAL PEACE AND
APPEAL TO THE PEOPLES OF THE WORLD THAT THE WISH BE ANSWERED PROMPTLY
MAY THE CHIME PERVADE THE REMOTEST CORNERS OF THE EARTH!
UNANIMOUS WITH ALL THE MEMBERS OF INTERNATIONAL LIONS CLUBS IN
STRIVING FOR THE GOAL, WE PRESENT THIS CLOCK TOWER TO THE MUNICIPALITY
AND THE CITIZENS.

OCTOBER 28, 1967 HIROSHIMA RIJO LIONS CLUB

PANEL 99   Here is one of the many moving peace messages posted
throughout the grounds of the Memorial Park described in
the previous PANEL.

The ruin of the prewar Industrial Hall in Hiroshima, a
landmark of the Atomic Bomb's "ground zero" is seen in
the background. In contrast, several pleasure boats are anchored in the placid stream at the very end of the large
War Memorial Park (1985). But this magnificent Memorial
is also a symbol of the most moving Gentle Way in Japan;
a unique blend of the prehistoric Shinto quest for renewal
and the ancient Buddhist concept of perpetual rebirth in a
pervasive yet serene plea for eternal peace.

Documentary Appendix

I.

THE PURPOSE of this Documentary Appendix is to give the reader some perception of both the new and the old Japan, to suggest what relation exists between them, and to place *Gentle Ways* in a clearer context. The Westerner who first arrives in Japan at Tokyo's modern Narita Airport may have little feeling that he is in the Far-East except for bilingual signs in Japanese/English and Oriental customs officers, a likely scenario in any major U.S. West Coast airport. If our traveller then takes a bus for the long trip to downtown Tokyo, he may notice the driver's spotless white gloves, the fresh-cut flowers in a small vase above his seat, the close-circuit TV to supplement the rear view mirrors and the soft stereo music piped through this immaculate vehicle riding smoothly on new super highways through farmland and countryside.

These peaceful early impressions gradually fade away at the outer reaches of Tokyo's sprawling megalopolis—its multitude of intertwined towns and smokestack cities; its interminable lines of densely packed new factories; its endless network of murky rivers and canals and train tracks interspersed with old neighborhoods of dark wooden houses along winding narrow lanes often wide enough for only one car, next to areas of concrete and blight and skyscrapers crisscrossed in all directions by more super highways. This extreme ugliness, in which no parcel of land however small is left unused, is compounded by unbelievable pollution, so severe at times that traffic policemen have had to breathe oxygen from a cannister every fifteen minutes, and children playing in schoolyards in heavily industrialized areas have had to wear gas masks.[1] Everyone remembers Minamata in the early sixties where organic mercury in raw sewage from chemical factories caused poisoning of fish, birds and animals leading in turn to ghastly and catastrophic deformities in the local population. Everyone remembers also "Tokyo-Yokohama asthma" in the fifties, a form of pneumonia due to air pollution which disabled tens of thousands. The situation has now somewhat improved but, just as in Los Angeles, it can be very critical on smoggy, steamy days.

It is this overwhelming industrial urban complex at the forefront of today's technology which typifies Japan Inc. and which the traveller first sees on his way to downtown Tokyo. Its monumental traffic jams, vast concrete office buildings and hotels, with huge crowds everywhere are some of the facets of intense urbanization which Courdy, an astute French critic, believes "is a permanent challenge to the mental equilibrium of individuals everywhere."[1]

Concern about the severe impact of industrialization and technology is not new. As early as 1914, Walter Lipmann remarked in *Draft and Mystery* that "We are not used to a complicated civilization, we don't know how to behave when personal contact and eternal authority have disappeared. . . . We have changed our environment more quickly than we have changed ourselves." Forty years later and shortly before his death, the great American philosopher George Santayana keenly observed that "Modern Technology has unhinged the human mind from its vital animal frame, and imposed on it a mad personal ambition. The great external success may easily involve an essential failure. But what if moral failure should pervade the experiment?" In 1970, Charles Reich, an apostle of the cultural revolution of the sixties, wrote: "The impact of technology, market and capitalism is written on our landscape, our culture, our faces. Perhaps the landscape shows it most vividly. . . . What happened to the land also happened to . . . the village community which was broken as we were forced to seek jobs in factories and cities. . . . The bonds of affection and concern between men were broken by the harsh imperatives of competition. . . . Man was uprooted from his physical and social environment, and like a polar bear in a city zoo, he would from then on suffer an alienated existence."[2]

Also in 1970, Alvin Toffler, a noted futurologist, emphasized that "the breakdown of human performance under heavy information load may be related to psychopathology in ways we have not yet begun to explore. . . . We are forcing people to process information at a far more rapid rate that was necessary in slow evolving societies . . . There are absolute limits to the amount of change that the human organism can absorb, and by endlessly accelerating change without first determining these limits, we may submit masses of men to demands they simply cannot tolerate."[3] Takeo Doi, one of Japan's foremost psychiatrists, writes: "Where man once felt pride in the modern civilization created by science and technology, he has now come to fear its ever-accelerating advances. He cherishes the suspicion that in return for (technological) civilization, he is deprived of something irreplaceable."[4]

In postwar Japan, observations on the social impact of the industrial world focus largely on the ill-effects of intense urbanization—to which 70% of all Japanese are subjected—and on "extreme overcrowding due to permanent lack of space." In this regard, former U.S. Ambassador's Reischauer classic text on the Japanese explains: "The speed of change encountered by all industrialized societies is greatest in Japan where the physical base is definitely worse. No country faces graver problems of crowding and . . . their standard of well-being is still relatively low. The Japanese lack adequate space for living, for diversion and for their business activities . . . and always will. The resulting high cost of land inflates all prices; crowding produces great economic waste through traffic congestion, pollution, long hours of painful commuting (3–6 hours a day for young people); . . . lack of space with cramped and relatively flimsy living quarters cuts down on the enjoyment of life . . . They are correct in their common complaint that they are in reality a lot poorer than statistics would indicate."[5]

Today, the housing problem appears to remain acute. Akio Mikuni, a prominent Tokyo financier, writes (*The Wall Street Journal*, November 16, '87): ". . . There should be huge investments in new homes for working people. . . . The Japanese live in 'rabbit hutches' and devote all their resources to export-oriented industry . . . I would like to see $150 billion to $200 billion thrust into building homes of an acceptable size . . ."

Courdy compares "horizontal" with "vertical" living quarters and underscores that "vertical living" in tall buildings "has been unsuccesful in all industrial countries where its development has promoted insecurity, loneliness and alienation together with a feeling of rejection and despair," leading to dehumanization, drugs, mental disorders, and finally a breakdown of the social fabric.[1] How then have the Japanese fared better in the climate of intense urbanization—where 70% of them live—than any other modern post-industrial technological nation? How then have they succeeded in the very midst of their exceedingly crowded cities to have considerably less crime, less juvenile delinquency, less divorces, less drugs, less AIDS, less moral and social disintegration than any other major industrial state? A perusal of Japan's group philosophy may provide a partial answer and can be considered in terms of the three cardinal features of Japanese life: harmony and homogeneity, persistence of traditional old structures, the group as a source of social and emotional security.[5,10]

II.

Homogeneity and Harmony: Homogeneity is primarily cultural, as there have been no significant population shifts into these islands for the past fifteen hundred years.[5,10] Chie Nakane, in her outstanding analysis of Japanese society, believes that the Tokugawa feudal system, which ruled Japan for nearly three centuries, added institutional homogeneity to the country's innate cultural homogeneity so that in spite of "the drastic changes suffered by Japanese society over the past hundred years . . . the basic social grammar has hardly been affected." A similar view had been expressed previously by Singer, a German philosopher in 1930,[11] and by Bellesort, a French Academician who lived in Japan before World War I and again in 1925.[12]

Harmony, on the other hand, was stressed "for all time to come as the key note of Life" by Prince Shotoku, the founding father of the Japanese state, in the first article of the State Code of Ethics written in the seventh century: "Harmony is to be valued and an avoidance of wanton opposition to be honored . . . All persons are influenced by class-feelings, and there are few who are intelligent . . . but when those above are harmonious and those below are friendly, and there is concord in the discussion of business, right views of

223

things spontaneously gain acceptance. What then is there that cannot be accomplished?"[11] Singer, in a penetrating study of Japanese life, tells us that Shotoku's Codes echo early Chinese teachings, and have been incorporated in the daily life of Japan to "make the stream of human intercourse flow gently . . . no one is allowed to stand on his own right and much less fight for it. Conflicts must be submitted for mediation and are solved by compromise . . ."[11] "Ethics blend into politeness," and an intricate set of reserves and constraints (*enryo*) toward everyone—close friends and family excepted—contribute to further harmony. The same is true for an ever-present sense of gratitude for past consideration or kindness (*on*), and for a deep sense of obligation due to favors received, no matter how small (*giri*).[5]

It is a generally held opinion that "the ways of Westerners in their daily life appear intolerably harsh to the Japanese; they see in Western intercourse—even among those who are friends—a perpetual giving and taking of blows and shocks."[11,5] In contrast there is the important and ubiquitous concept of *amae* in Japanese life. *Amae*, the infant's desire for motherly love and attention has come to mean in adult life "to look to the other for affection"[4,5] or to give and hope for caring empathy. It should be emphasized, however, that when they are with foreigners where the "quasi-magical force of rite and custom does not prevail," the Japanese at times may loose their "ethical bearings,"[5] and "may speak or act with dangerous arbitrariness and discourtesy."[11] Similar loss in "ethical bearing" during war or totalitarian rule may result in massacres and extreme cruelty. Unfortunately the same applies to many other nations.

Persistence of old, traditional social structures:　As Singer describes it so well, Japan is a "distinctly non-urban country: The most persistent and some of the most valuable features of Japanese society, even today, are legacies of rural life. . . . Even in the town you will find the countryside, says an old Japanese proverb."[11] The hub of large cities may be a modern section built near a famous old castle as in Tokyo; or a grid pattern of avenues and streets built on the Chinese model in the seventh century first in Nara then in Kyoto; or again an amorphous amalgam of concrete towers and squares in newly rebuilt postwar cities as in Hiroshima, Nagoya and many others. Yet in every case, these central areas are surrounded by a "cluster of villages grown to immoderate dimensions."[11] While increasingly more Japanese are now urbanized, the rural population has fallen from 60% in 1945 to 10% in 1970 and 5% in 1986. Yet most city people continue to think like the Japanese of long ago.[1,10] This has been repeatedly noted by many observers, both Japanese and foreign, since industrialization began in 1868 at the onset of the Meiji period. Tokyo was almost burned to the ground in 1923 after the big earthquake and once again after intense fire bombing in World War II, and yet on both occasions many parts of the city were rebuilt on the old pattern of feudal times.[1]

It is within this rural framework that the basic social structure of Japan, the household (or *ie*) first arose, probably in the first centuries of this era. Nakane gives a lucid analysis of such households: "A small group of a dozen or less people comprising family and retainers" was found to function best. Individuals of different status were not separated but formed an integral group with marriages often occurring among them. This contributed to "blur lines of distinction" and to establish what Nakane calls "a single vertical bond in social relationship between individual and group," with all sharing "basic equality and communal rights." In such a group, "overt stratification is not recognized but delicately graded ranking" is perceived by all. The individual household thus became stronger than kinship itself. An association of several households formed a village and one or several villages formed a *mura*. A binding sense of solidarity thus became the goal for each small rural community."[10] All decisions in the households or villages or even *muras* were made by consensus, and everyone—no matter how modest his condition—could have his say. On a different plane, a lord and his vassals operated on identical principles: Formation of a single household with "ranking but no overt stratification."[10,5]

Within all groups there existed a time honored senior-junior relationship, which is still primary today everywhere in Japan; it became the patron-client (*oyabun-kobun*) relationship central to any dealings in

Japanese society. Of almost equal importance as an expression of solidarity are age-groups where persons of the same age form bonds which may last a lifetime. With the gradual erosion of family life present in all post-industrial nations, it is only in Japan that the ancient familial group began to be replaced with the company or firm as the "provider of the whole social existence of a person . . . A company is now conceived as a household, with all its employees qualifying as members and the employer as its head. Thus, the basic and ancient social structure persists in Japan in spite of great changes in social organization."[10,5]

The "dense social matrix of small society relationships"[11] within the framework of the workplace viewed as a group, continues to protect its members as in former times, but it now sustains them against the alienation and other dehumanizing effects of technological civilization. Singer observed sixty years ago what Nakane and others have emphasized recently, that the "durability of the fundamental pattern of personal relationships has scarcely been touched by modernization."[10,5,1] While the formal structure of a Japanese corporation or production unit is the same as in the West, the informal structure differs greatly: It is founded on the "dense social matrix" of personal relationship which derives from the "one-to-one vertical type of relationship between patron and client, junior and senior, professor and student alumni of a same school, and so on." It is perhaps Nakane's central thesis that this peculiar type of Japanese hierarchy within the company's informal group structure is at the root of Japan's economic miracle. It has been "the driving force of Japan's industrial development and has brought greater success than any other type of organization, as it is a reflection of basic national values closely linked to the overall social organization of the country."[10] For the same reasons, the Western type of horizontal organization, with everyone competing with everyone else, has had little success in Japan, where such behavior goes against the grain of the national character and is believed to breed nepotism with the constant danger of take-over by one group or another.[10]

The Group as a source of social and emotional security:
The Japanese concept that "the most effective results in group operation come from total group effort, and not from the net contributions of its individual members" is alien to the Western mind which emphasizes individual performance. In contrast, the Japanese have long believed that a person's mental attitude and emotional well-being within the group were "fundamental to his productive power." Management is constantly striving to develop a "cohesive sense of group unity" where the individual would feel as a "member of a family with full emotional participation in the group." For example, not only do managers and employees regularly eat together in the company's cafeteria, but to some extent the employer may participate in his subordinates' private lives. Thus he would be welcome—as would a relative—at major events in the employee's life: wedding, births, funerals. Some retired executives even give their time to counsel company employees.[10] In the West, such efforts would be decried as paternalistic, but within a highly homogeneous society, they seem to have succeeded. Not only is everything done to make the employee feel a valued member of the group, but more important perhaps—every effort is made not to hurt his feelings; and it is this respect toward the individual which will further enhance his devotion to the company.

Reischauer, who was born in Japan and lived there many years, has a full appreciation of everyday life and of the nuances of mutual regard and consideration in effect in the workplace:[5] Efforts are continually made to develop a "warm sense of personal loyalty" between management and employees; wages increase according to seniority only; lifetime employment is maintained since the early Meiji period in order to insure a steady supply of specialized workers; "no one is asked to work under a person of the same graduating class or younger, and when one man of a given class in an organization reaches the top post, all others of the same class retire . . . there is no competition across age or status lines" and harmony can be maintained, which is further enhanced by close cooperation between government and business.[5] This system is by no means idyllic[5,1] and some may think it is both archaic and inefficient, but most Japanese thrive on it and its overall reward in goodwill and performance is unmatched anywhere. There is, however, "complete estrangement"

225

of those outside the group, yet the excluded ones are relatively few for a nation of 120 million: First, there are "day-workers" without a steady job and thus no group benefits; next there is a small but growing number of unemployed. Then there are Koreans who have lived in Japan for generations but have always been set apart and suspected, if not accused outright, of any and all crimes; the Burakumin who are pure Japanese, but who since antiquity have been ostracized because of their occupation in the tanning and butchering businesses, once proscribed by Buddhism; lastly all foreigners who—as their name *gaijin* indicates—are "people from the outside" and can never really be included.[1] The same usually applies to any very homogenous group or nation. Still, the destitute in Japan form quite a small percentage at the bottom, as do the super-rich at the top, while the percentage of the middle class is probably one of the world's highest.[1,5]

III.

The paramount consideration, in any Japanese company is close human relations within one's work group. In such a setting, the position of the leader is an important one: He knows that "a company with good human relations will have incentives and will succeed in its business."[10] He knows, and this is crucial, that human beings live in an inimical world and need the constant reassurance of an emotionally secure environment to perform well. This is why Japanese leaders and managers are committed "to a high degree of involvement in personal relationships" with their employees. In order to achieve this, a "leader must hold his men emotionally and fulfill their expectations. He must understand and attract his men . . . He must protect them, and such protection is repaid by dependence, affection, loyalty . . . In Japan, the leader's raison d'etre is to serve as a pivot for human relationship and keep the peace . . . He must at times accept his men's opinion, even when inferior to his own, so as to enhance his men's importance."[10]

These executives are no more brilliant and technically competent than Western ones, neither do they make more money. While some may receive very high perks, they have generally much lower salaries and far simpler residences than their Western counterparts. But the Japanese managers' most valuable asset, and perhaps the key to their huge success, is their personal involvement with the emotional well being and satisfaction at work of their employees. This unique personal relationship between managers and their subordinates is in sharp contrast with the class societies still discernible in Western democracies, where there is often an abyss between the top executives and ordinary workers.[5,10] In sum then, Japanese employees within the work group are treated as valued members of an extended family, and not—which is still frequent in the West—as individuals to whom management "owes a day's wage for a day's work" and nothing more.[13]

Selected Bibliography

1. Courdy, Jean Claude: *Les Japonais: La vie de tous les jours dans l'empire du Soleil Levant*, Pierre Belfond, Paris, 1979
2. Reich, Charles: *The Greening of America*, Random House, New York, 1970
3. Toffler, Alvin: *Future Shock*, Random House. New York, 1970
4. Doi, Takeo: *The Anatomy of Dependence*, Kodansha International, Tokyo, New York and San Francisco, 1981
5. Reischauer, Edwin O.: *The Japanese*, Harvard University Press, 1977
6. Picken, Stuart, D.B.: *Shinto: Japan's Spiritual Roots*, Kodansha International, Tokyo, New York and San Francisco, 1980
7. Greenhall, Agnes and Levey, Judith, editors: *Columbia Encyclopedia*, Columbia University Press, 1950
8. Awakawa: *Zen Painting*, Kodansha International, Tokyo, 1970
9. Picken, Stuart, D.B.: *Buddhism: Japan's Cultural Identity*, Kodansha International, Tokyo, New York and San Francisco, 1982
10. Nakane, Chie: *Japanese Society*, Weidenfeld and Nicolson, London, 1970
11. Singer, Kurt: *Mirror, Sword and Jewel: The Geometry of Japanese Life*, Kodansha International. Tokyo, New York and San Francisco, 1973
12. Bellesort, André: *Le nouveau Japon*, Perrin & Co., Paris 1926
13. Carter, Hodding, III: "Economic Success has its Cost", *The Wall Street Journal*, p. 19, August 27, 1987
14. Bownas, Geoffrey: *Climate, a Philosophical Study*, Tokyo 1961, (Translation of Watsuji's "Fudo" quoted by R. Storry in Ref. 11.)
15. Malraux, André: *La condition humaine*, Gallimard, Paris, 1946.
16. Hearn, Lafcadio: *Selected Writings*, edited by Henri Goodman, The Citadel Press, New York, 1959 (Folk Culture: "A Woman's Diary" p. 471, and Essays: "Of the Eternal Feminine", pp. 506–515)
17. de Gramont, Sanche: *The French, Portrait of a People*, Putnam's Sons, New York, 1969
18. Ford, Barbara: Introduction in *Japanese Ink Painting: Early Zen Masterpieces*, by Kanazawa, H., Kodansha International & Shibundo, Tokyo, New York & San Francisco, 1979
19. Smith, Bradley: *Japan, a History in Art*, Doubleday Windfall New York, 1964
20. Japan Travel Bureau: *Japan: the Official Guide*, Tokyo 1954.
21. Landy, P: *Japon: Encyclopedie de Voyage*, Nagel, Geneva, Paris and Munich, 1973
22. Picken, Stuart, D.B.: *A Handbook of Shinto*, Tsubaki Grand Shrine of America, 1987
23. Reischauer, Edwin O.: Introduction, to Picken's *Shinto: Japan's Spiritual Roots*. Op. Cit. Ref. 6.
24. Ienaga, Saburo: *Japanese Art, A Cultural Appreciation*, Weatherhill/Heibonsha, New York, Tokyo 1979
25. Mosher, Gouverneur: *Kyoto, A Contemplative Guide*, Charles E. Tuttle Company, Publishers, Rutland and Tokyo, 1984
26. Haga, Hideo and Warner, George, Dr.: *Japanese Festivals*, 2nd edition, Hoikusha Publishing Co., Osaka 1969.

About the Author

GERARD P. SHELDON was born in Switzerland in 1923. He was educated in that country, in France and in the United States. He holds degrees from Harvard (S.B. '45) and from the University of Geneva (M.D. '51). From 1953 to 1956, he served as a U.S. Navy physician in Korea with the First Marine Division and in Japan, at the Yokosuka Naval Hospital. It was then that he first developed his life-long interest in Japanese life and art. Upon discharge from Naval active duty, he completed his training in San Francisco, and has practiced Internal Medicine and Chest Diseases in that city since 1958. He is married to the former Kana Hirooka, a painter and flower arranger from Kyoto, Japan. They have lived in Tiburon on San Francisco Bay since 1956. They have no children but share their home with a Golden Retriever and two alley cats. The author's spare time is taken up by travel, photography, writing and some epicurean pursuits. This is his first book.